I0512799

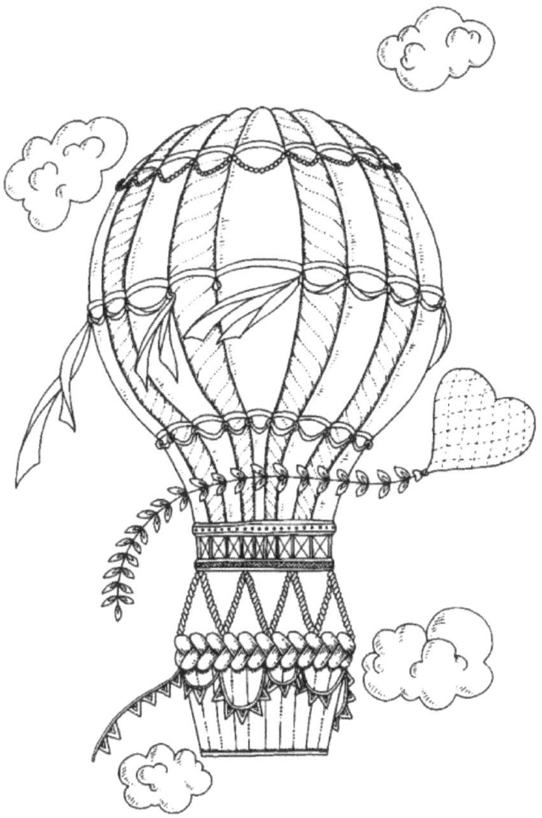

BALLOON PUBLISHING

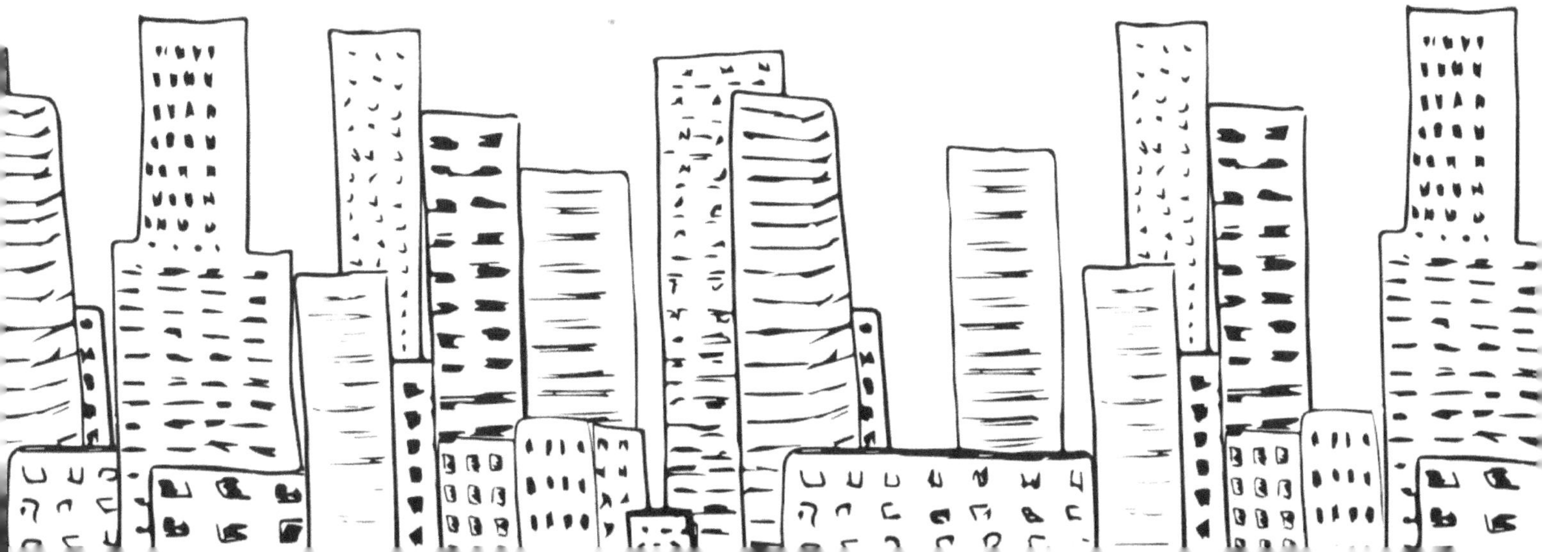

COLOR TEST PAGE

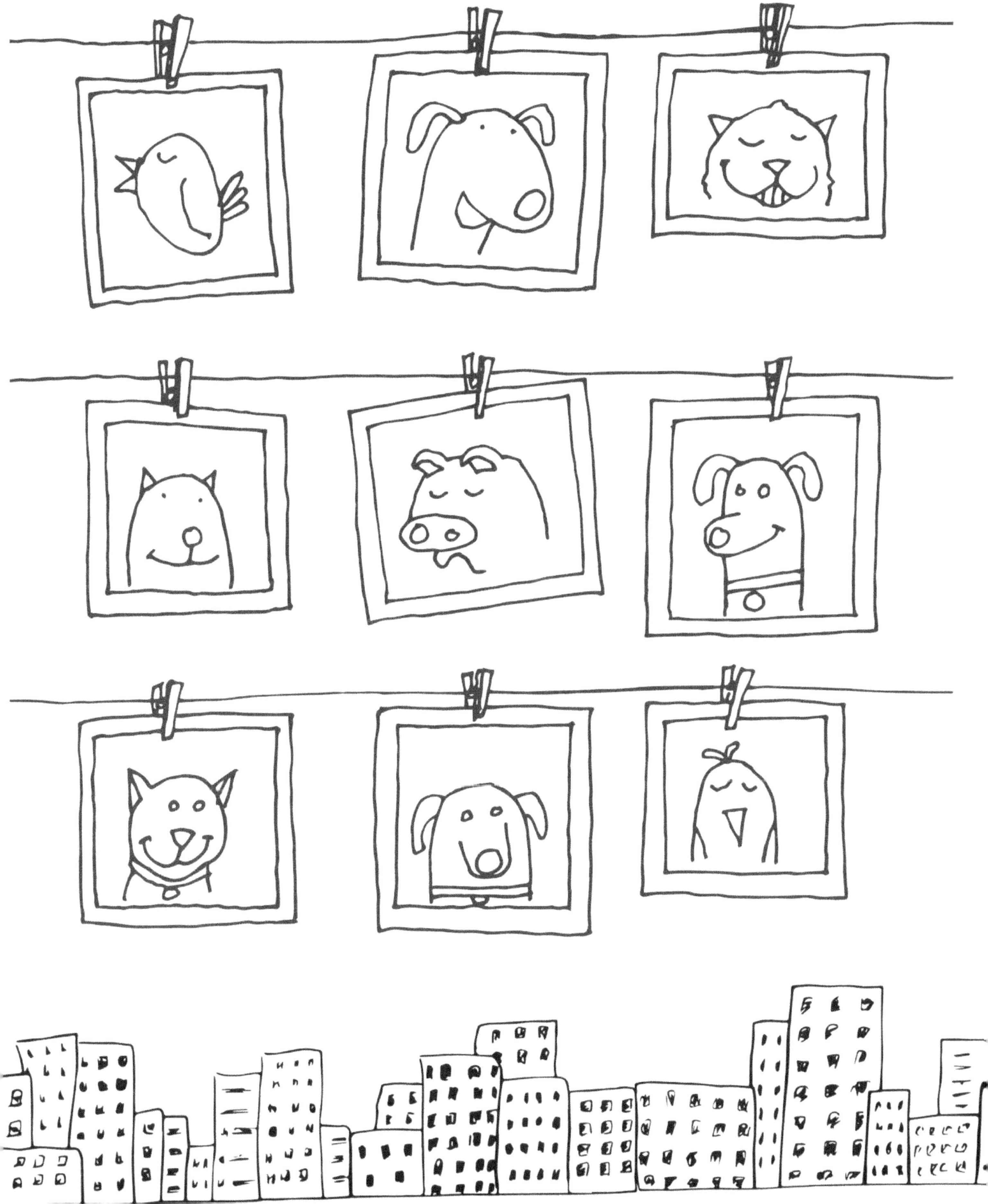

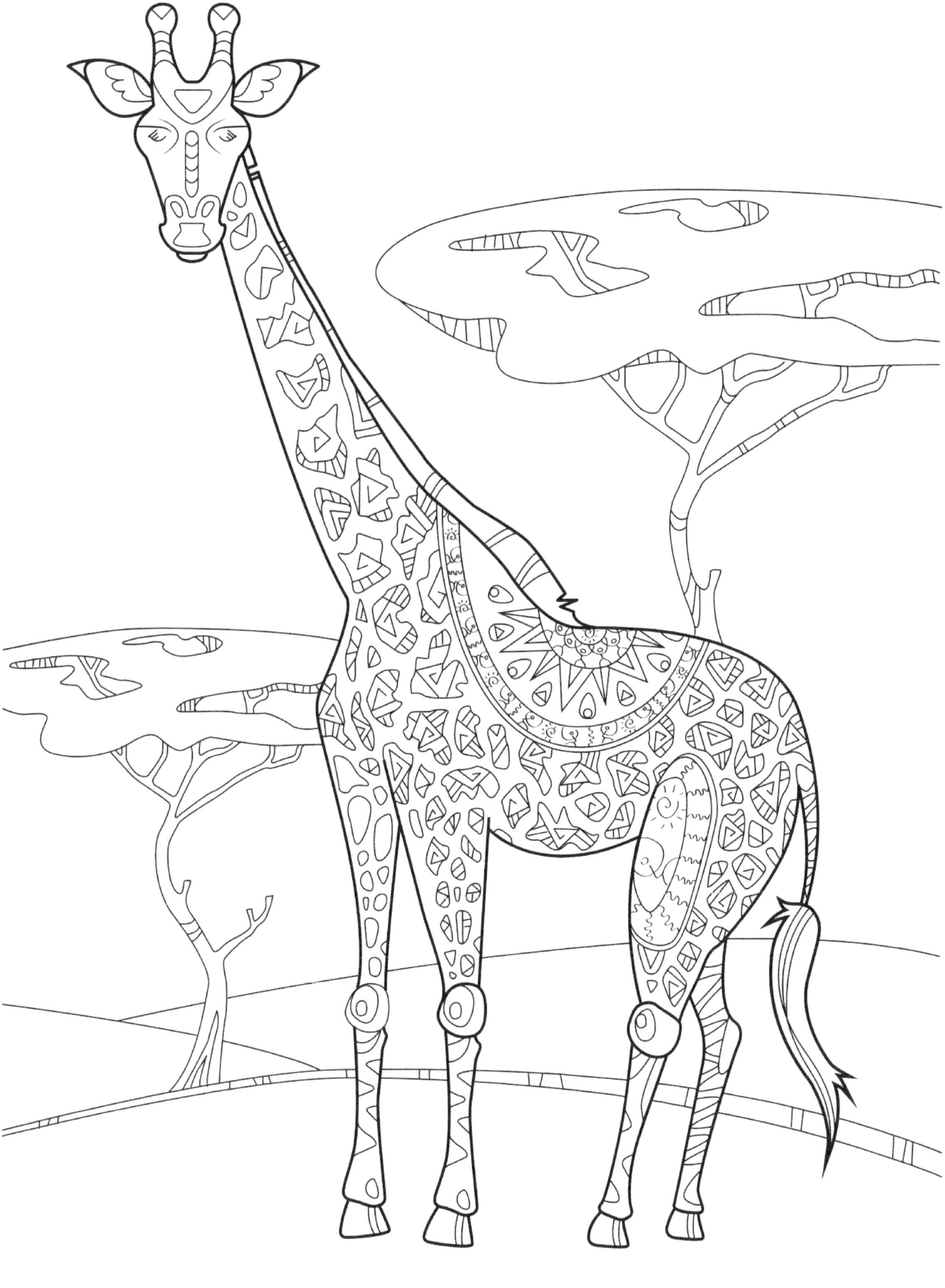

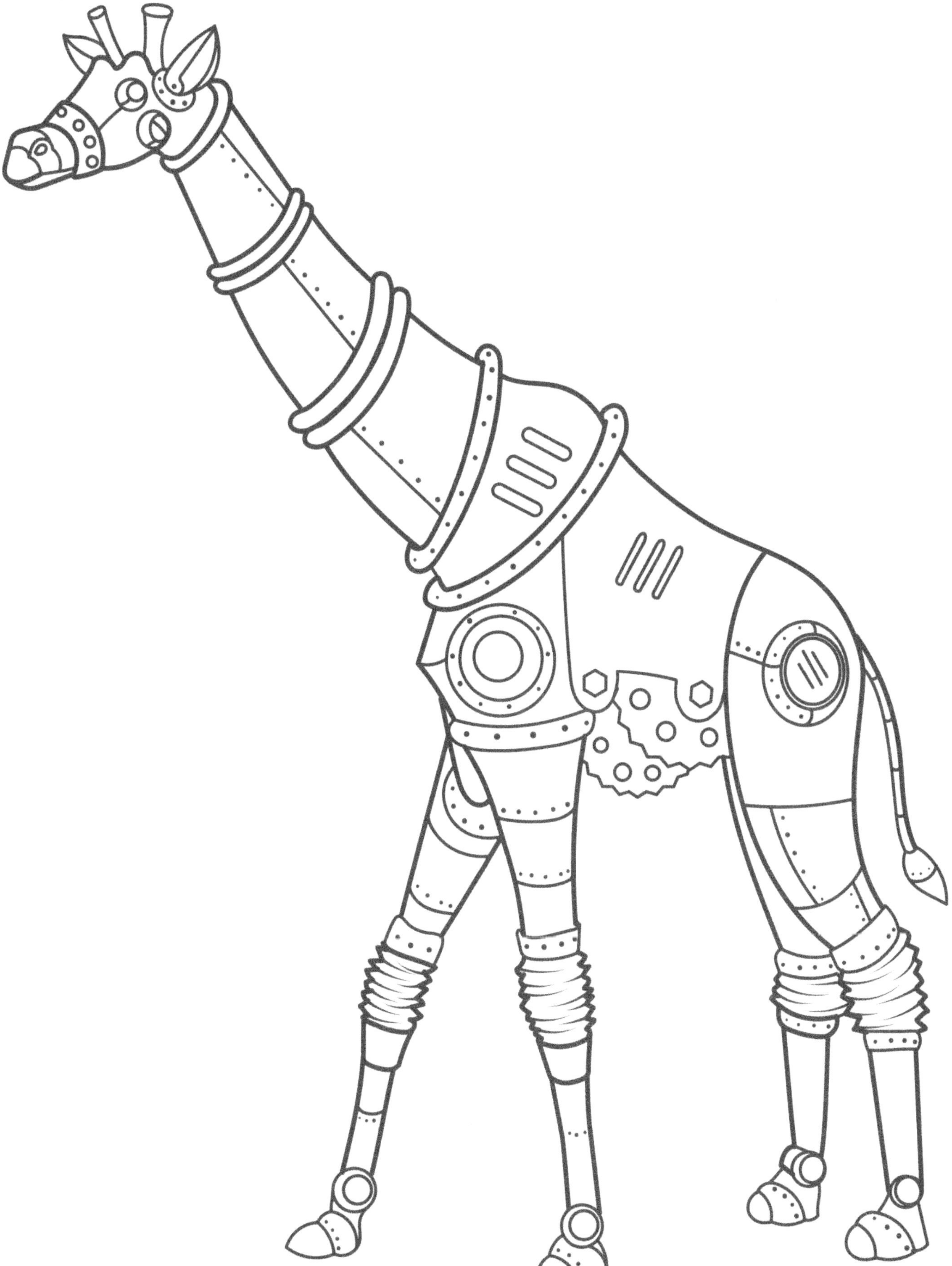

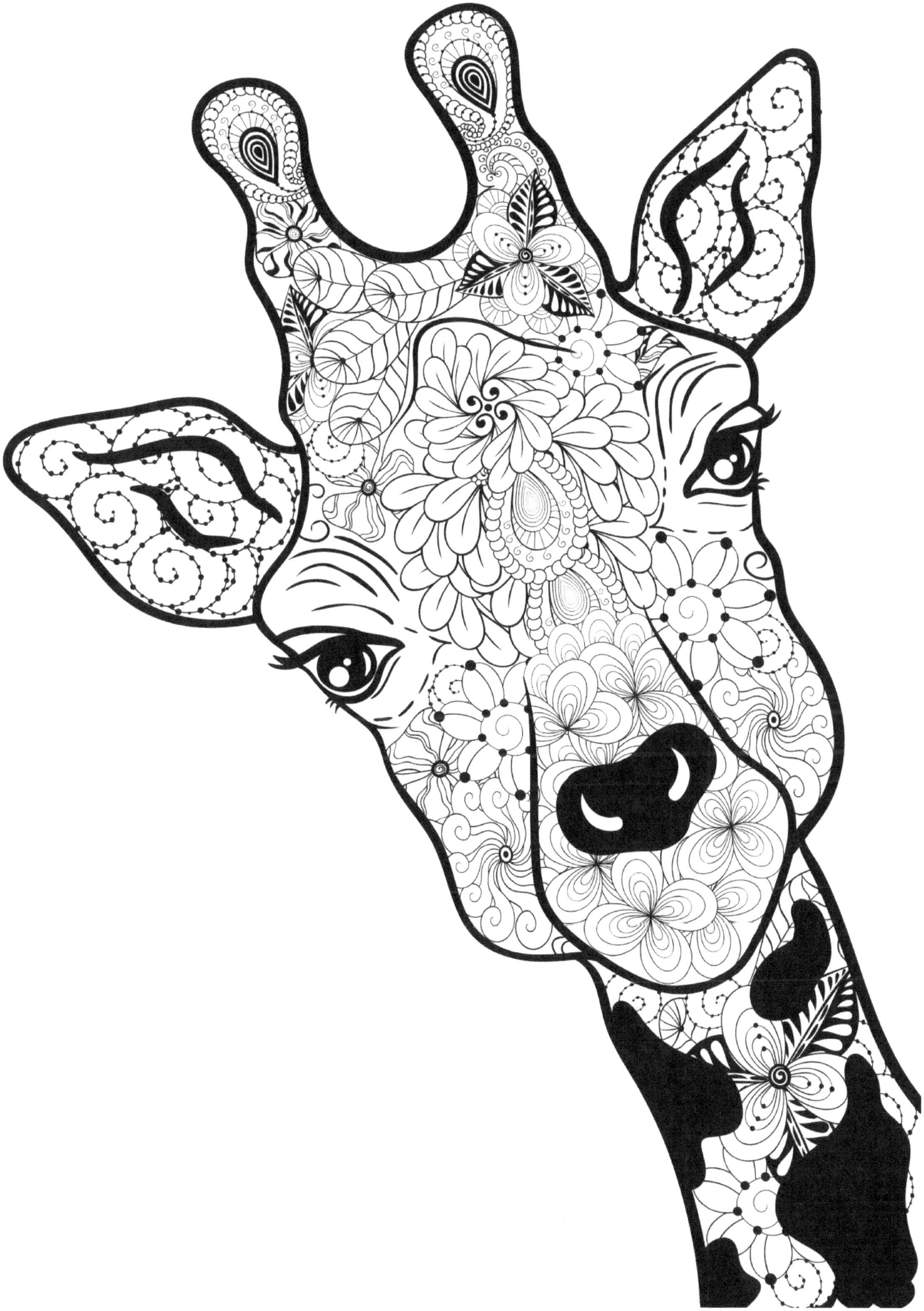

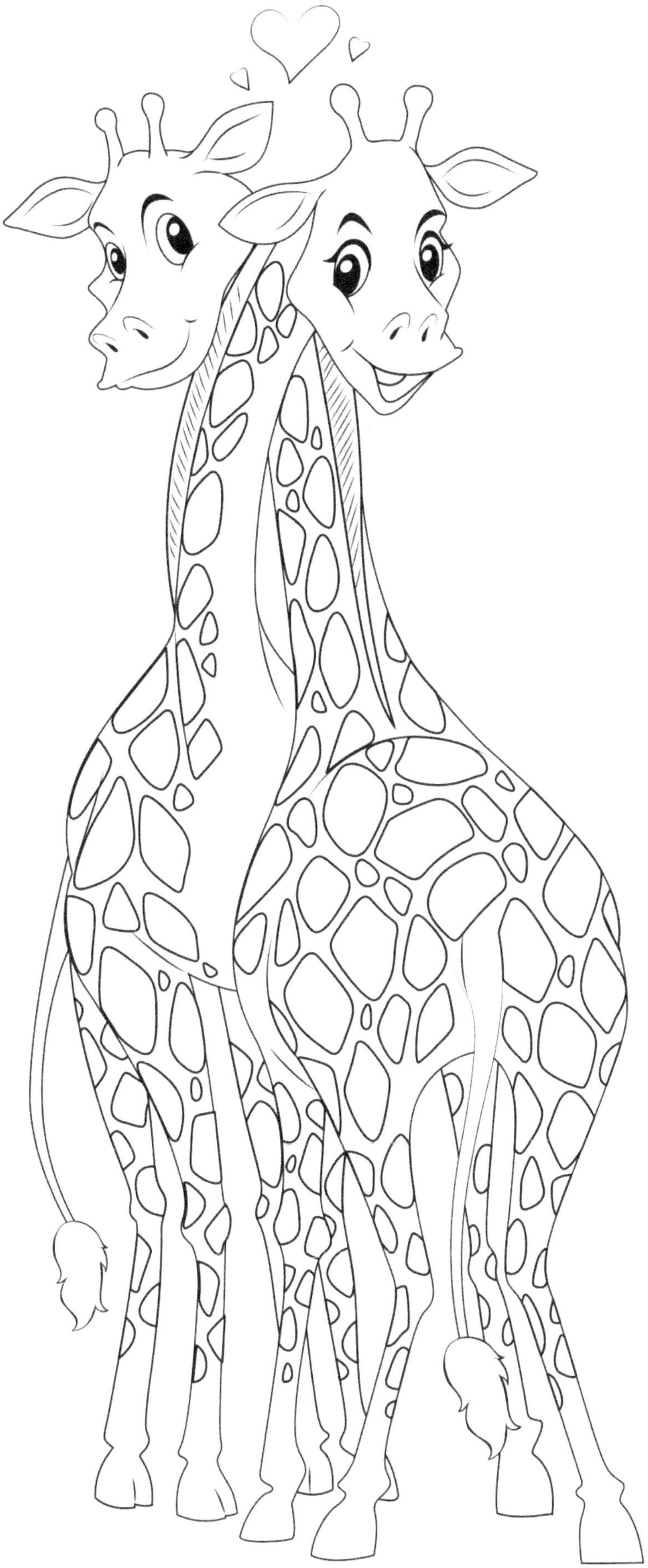

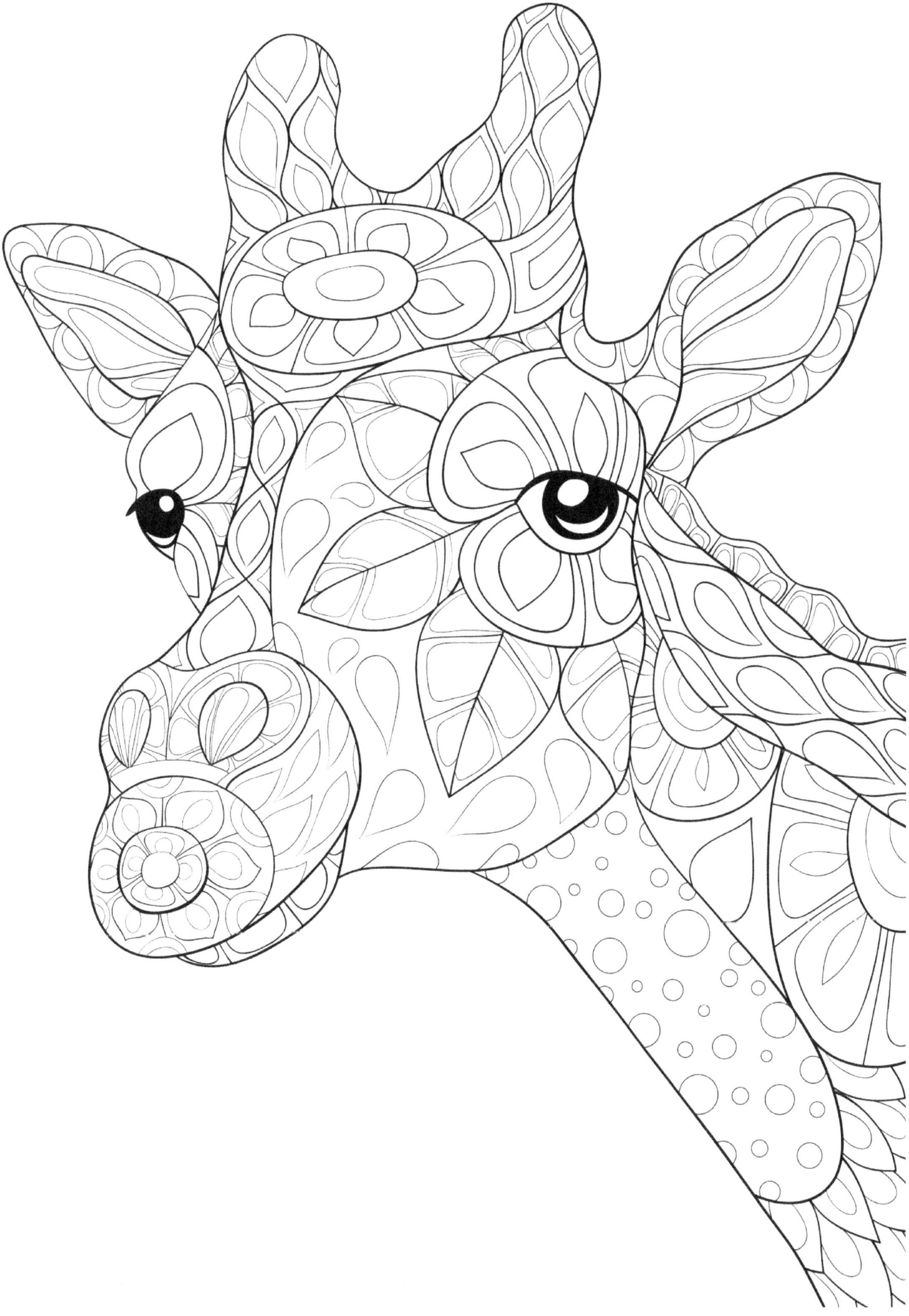

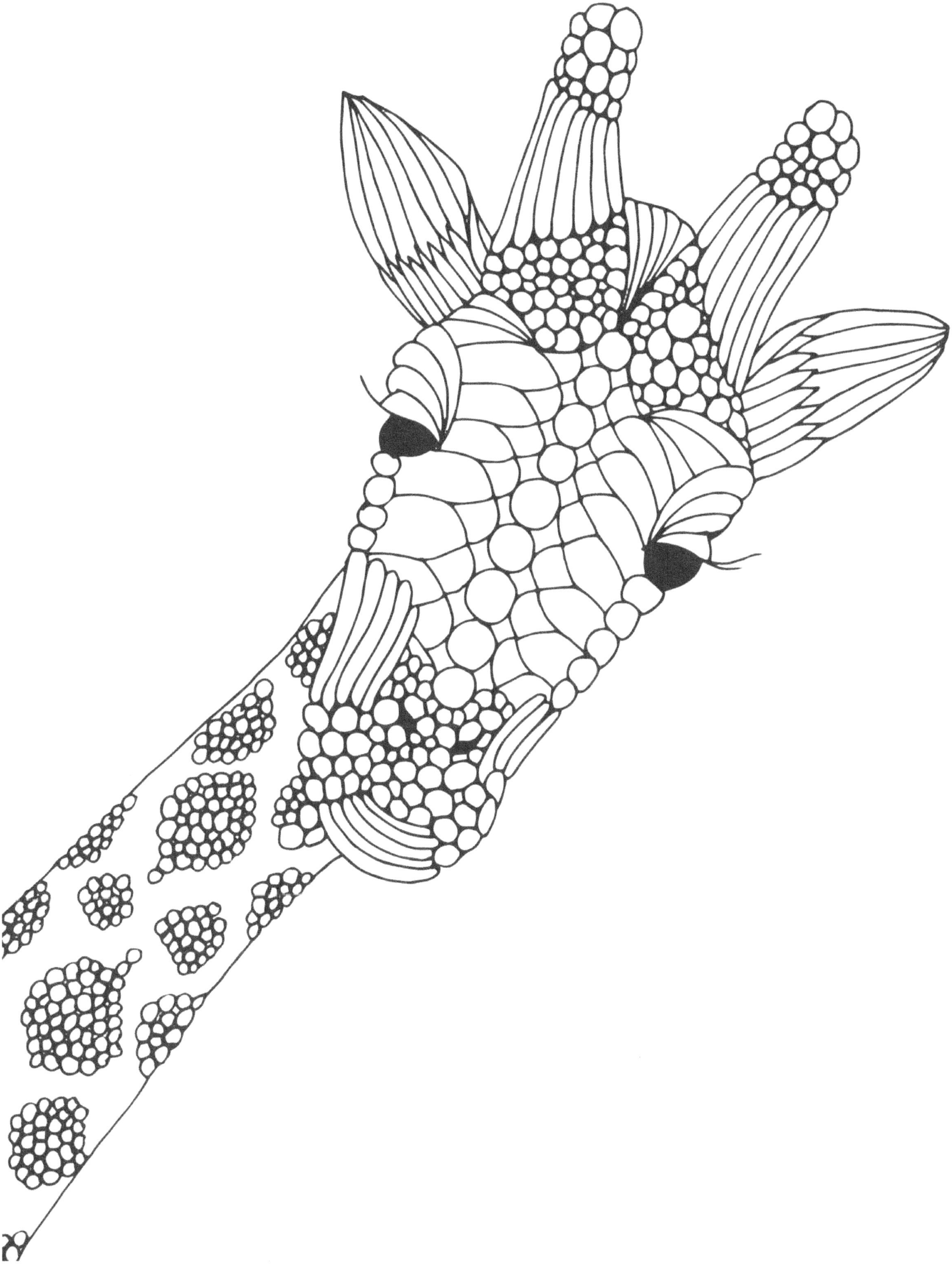

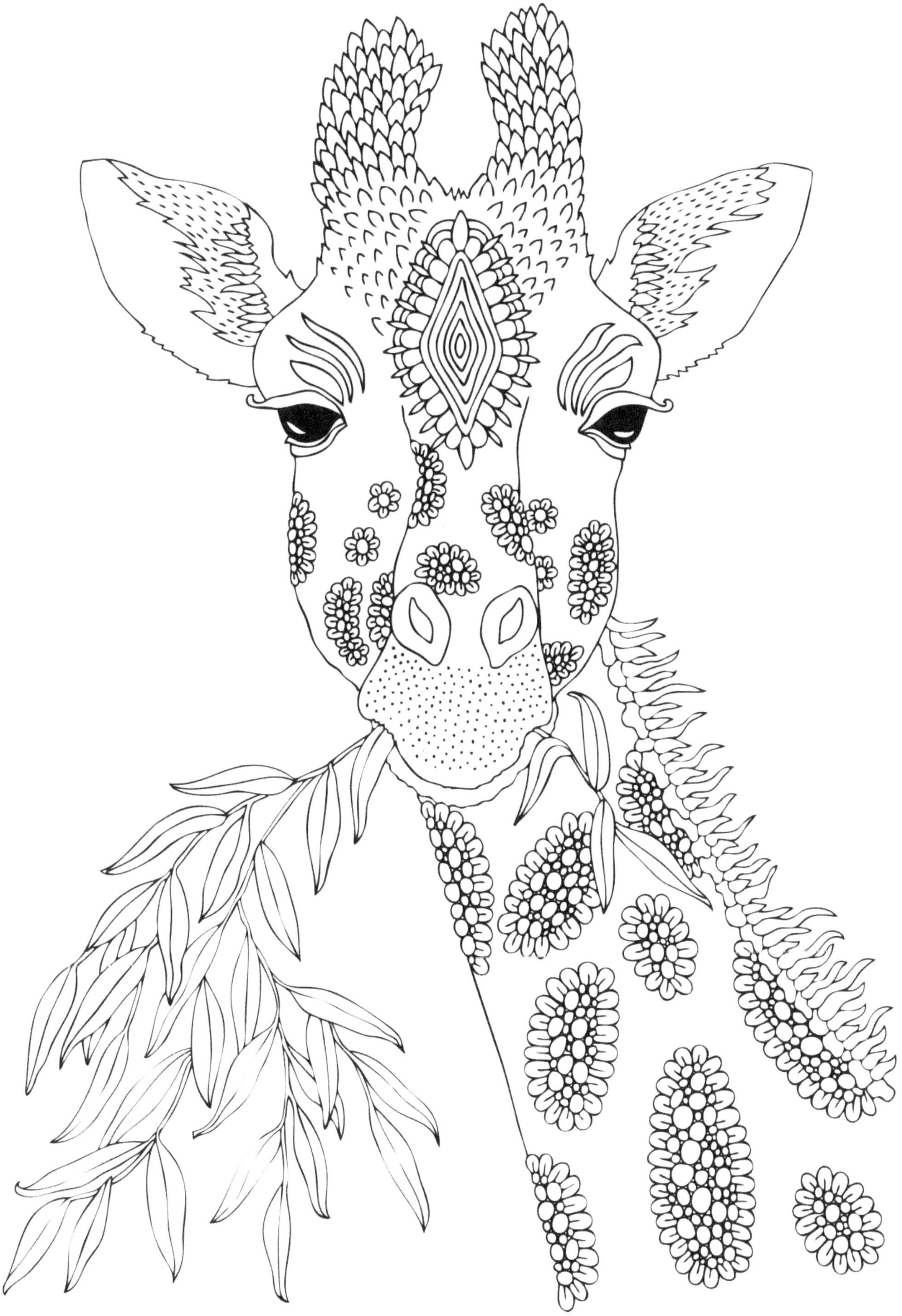

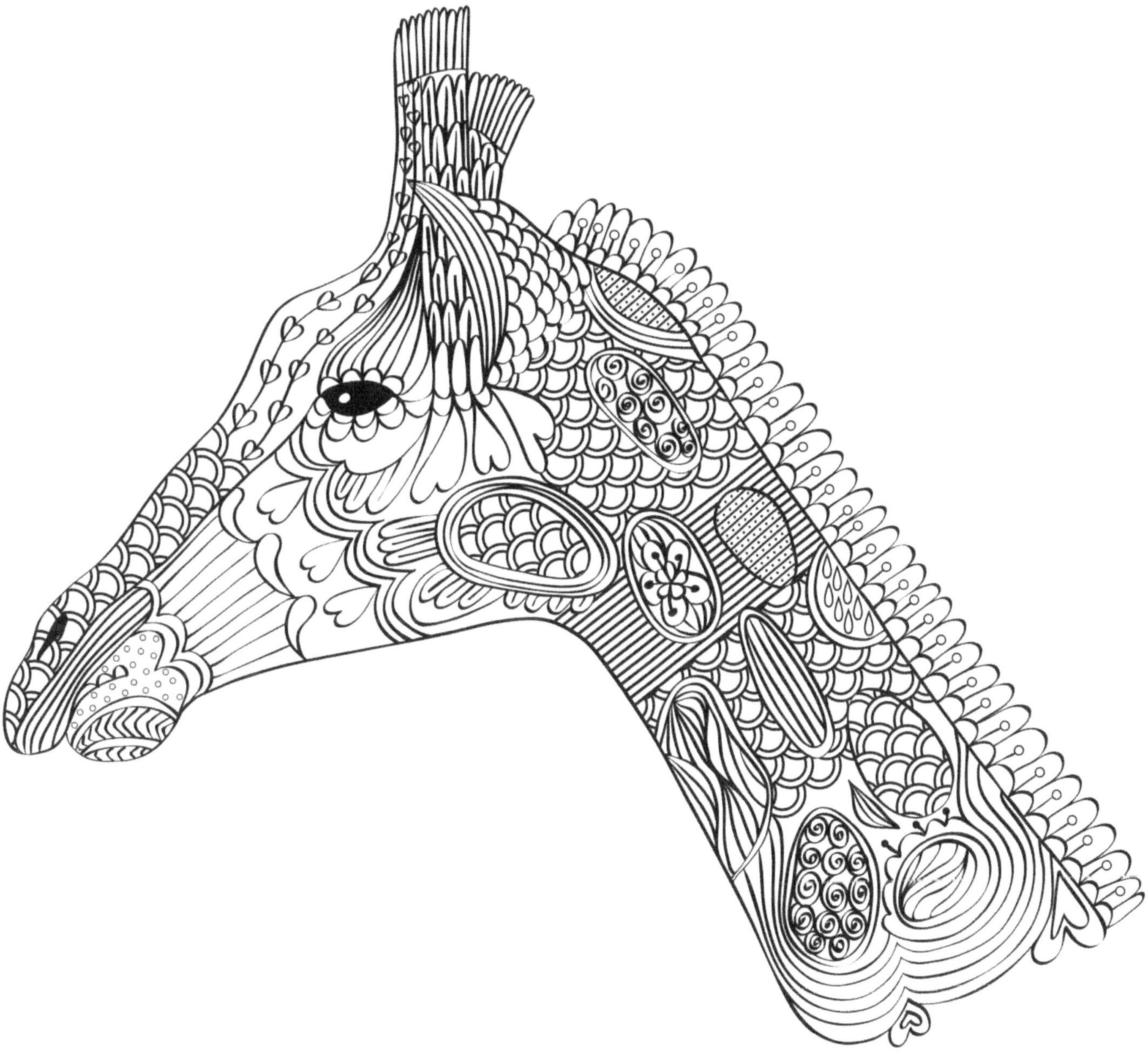

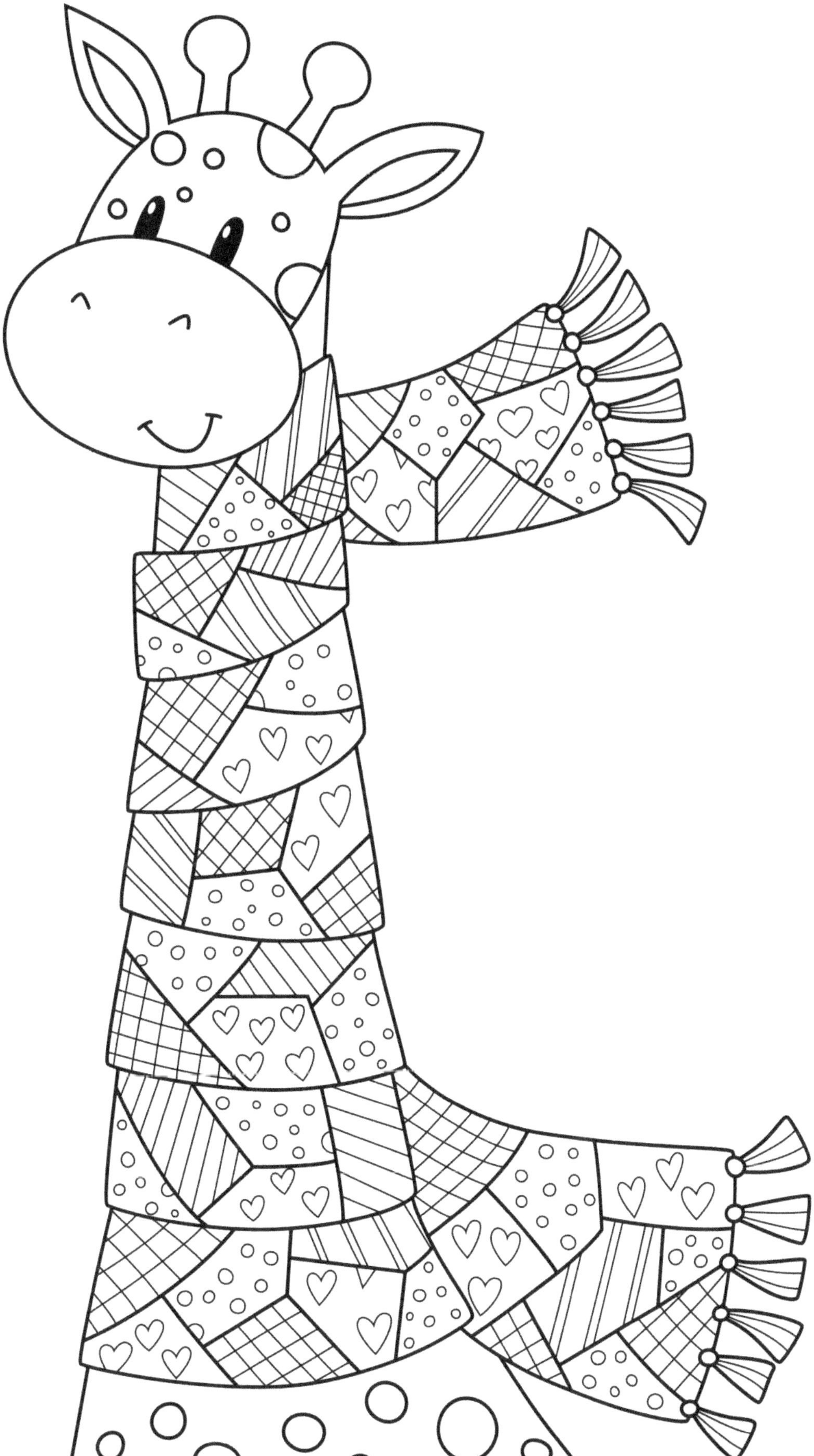

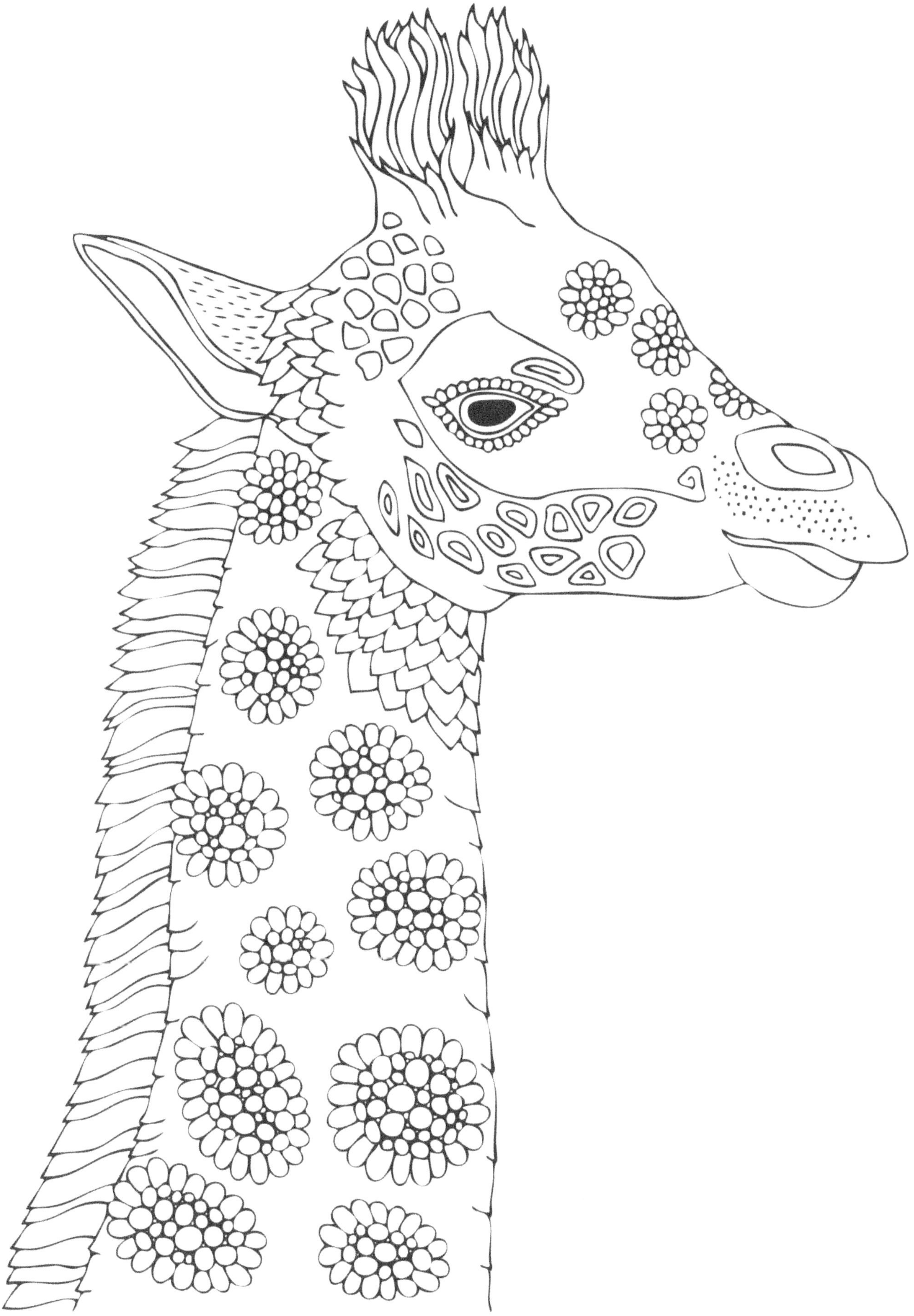

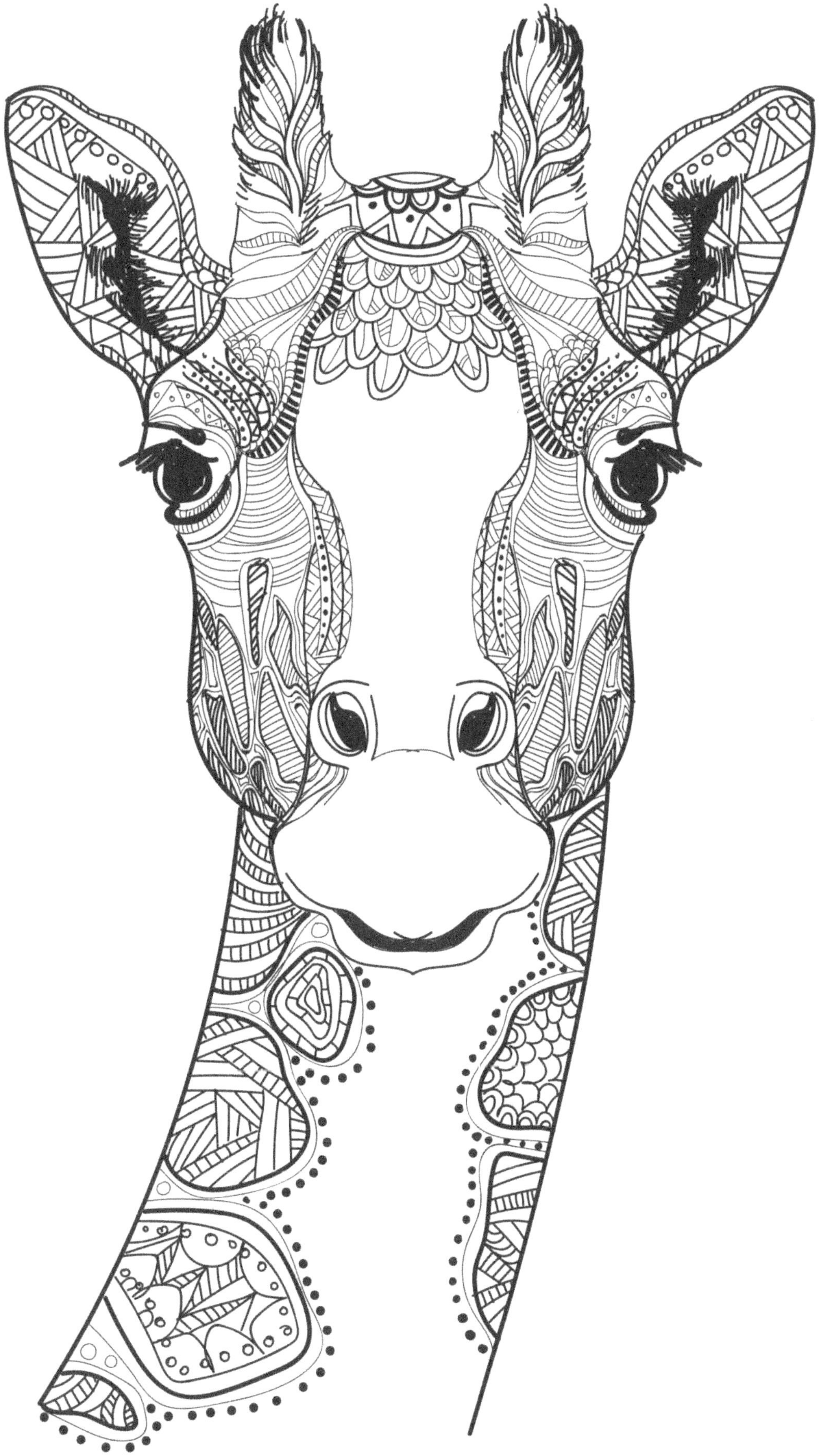

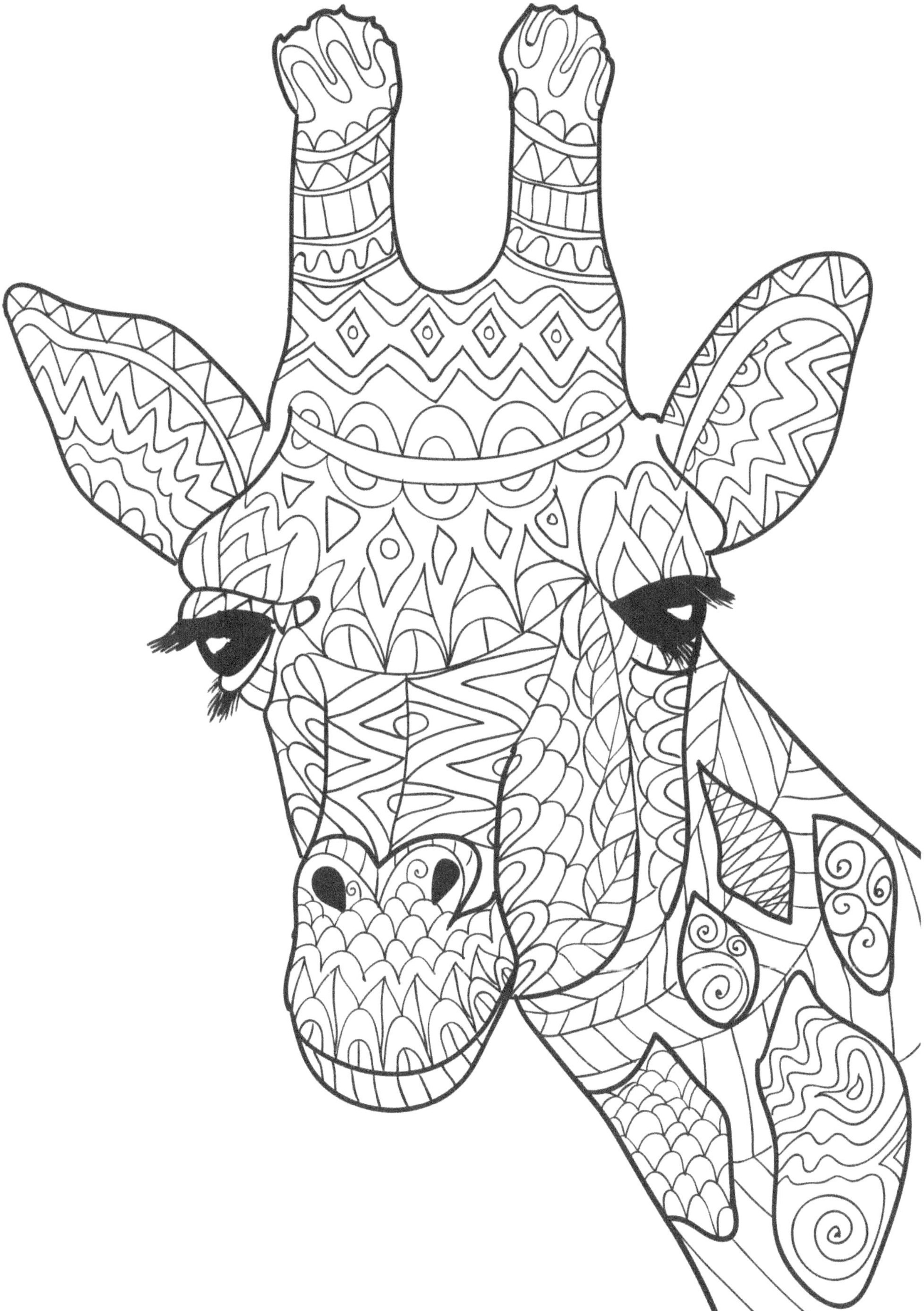

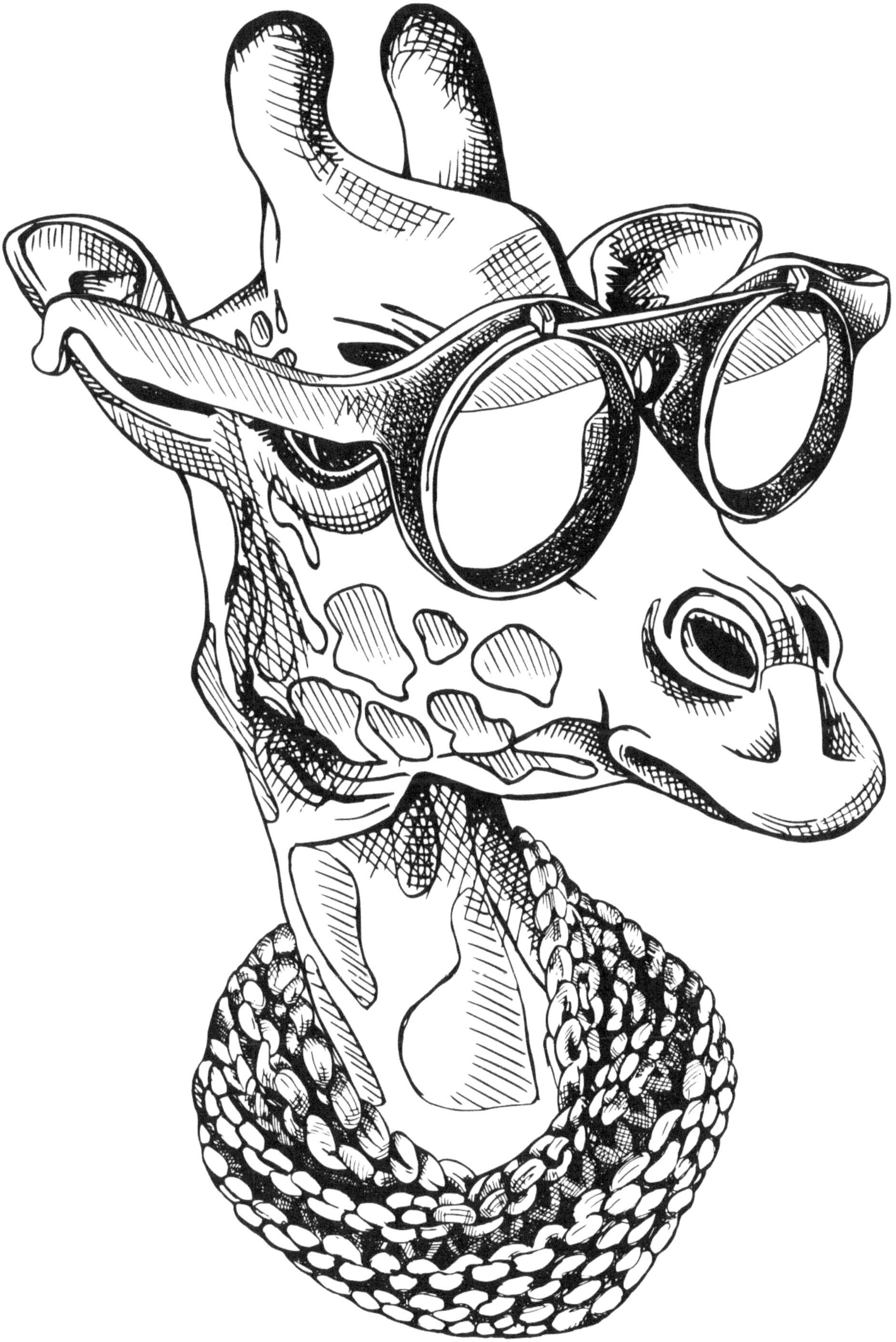

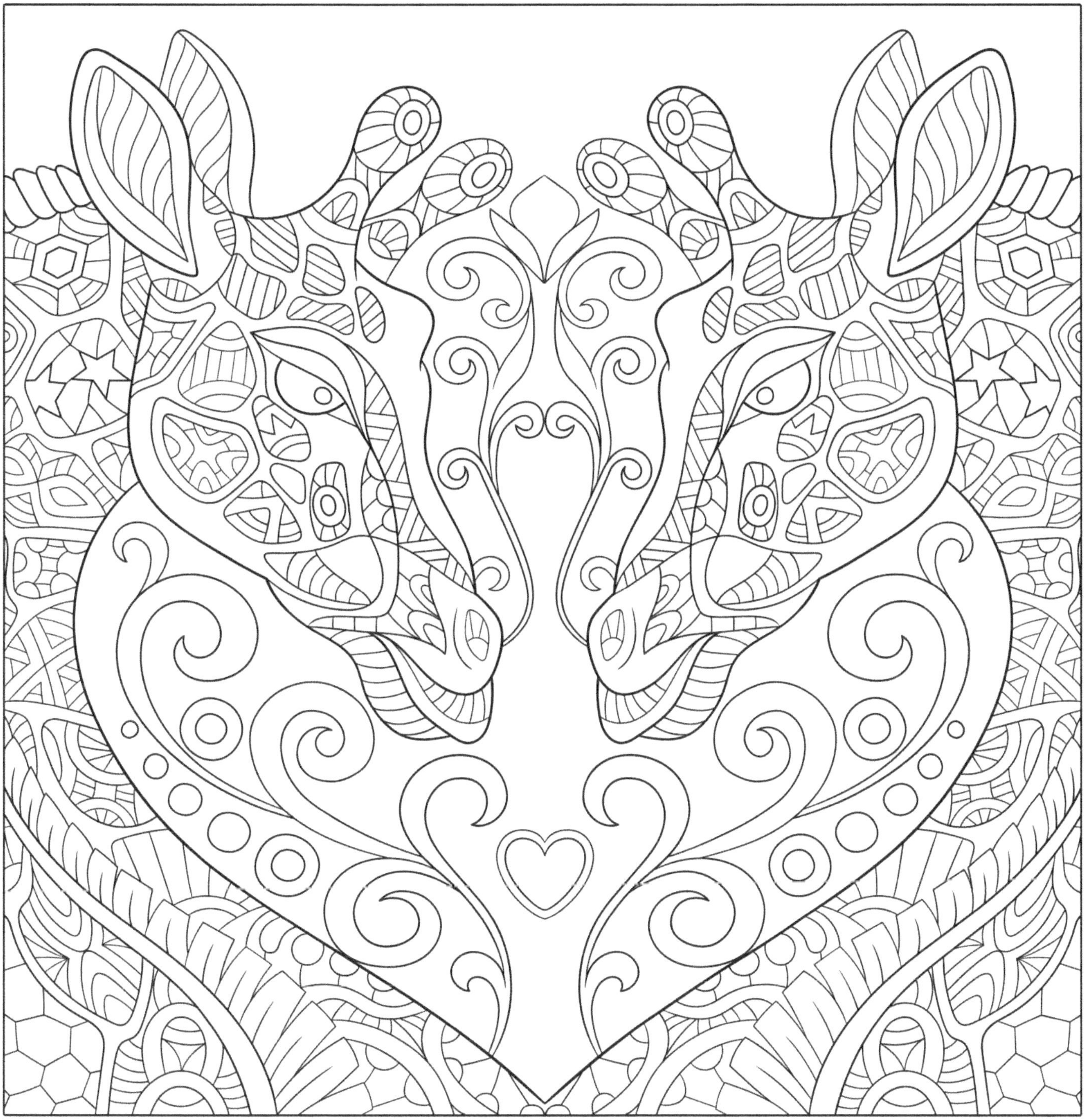

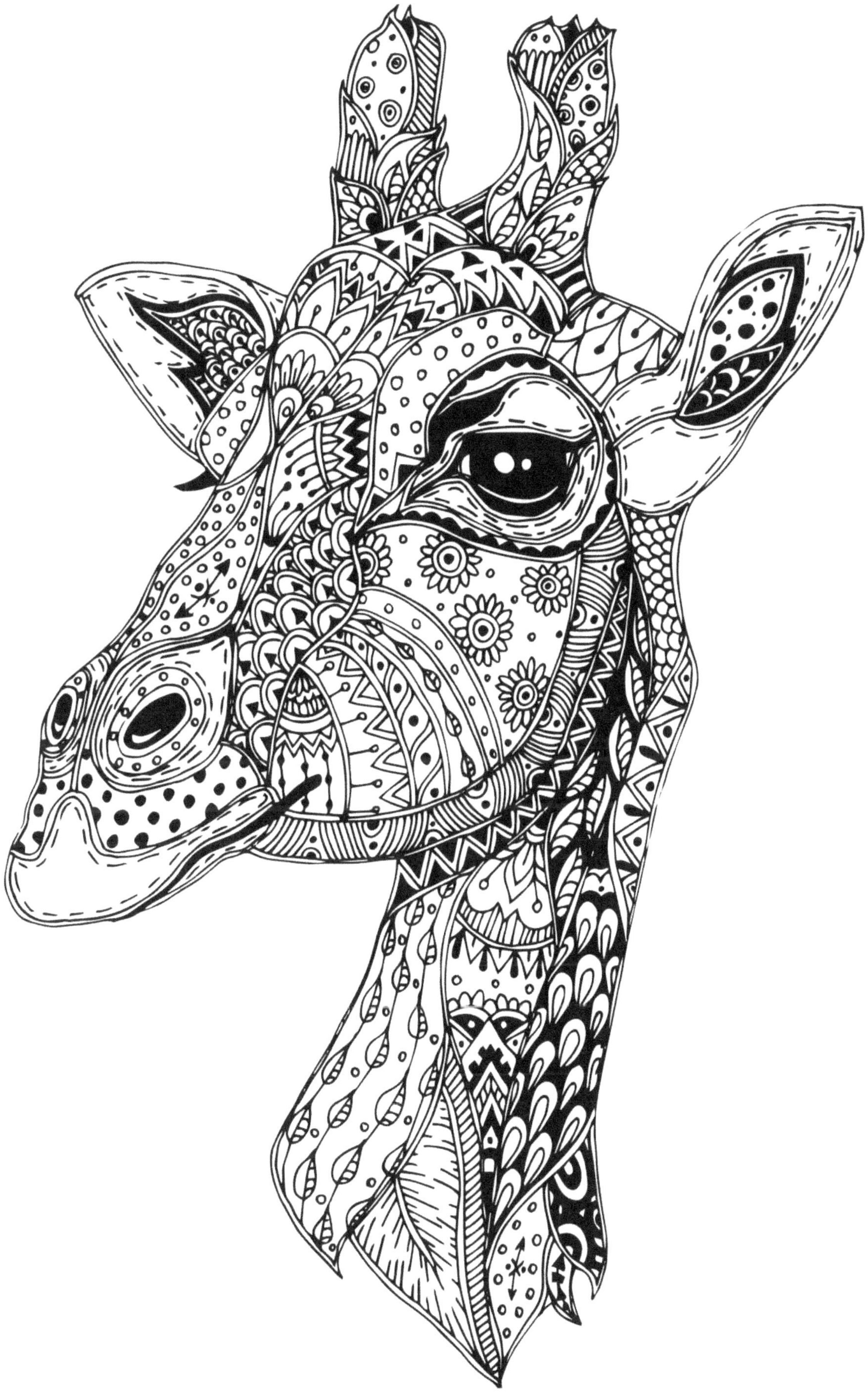

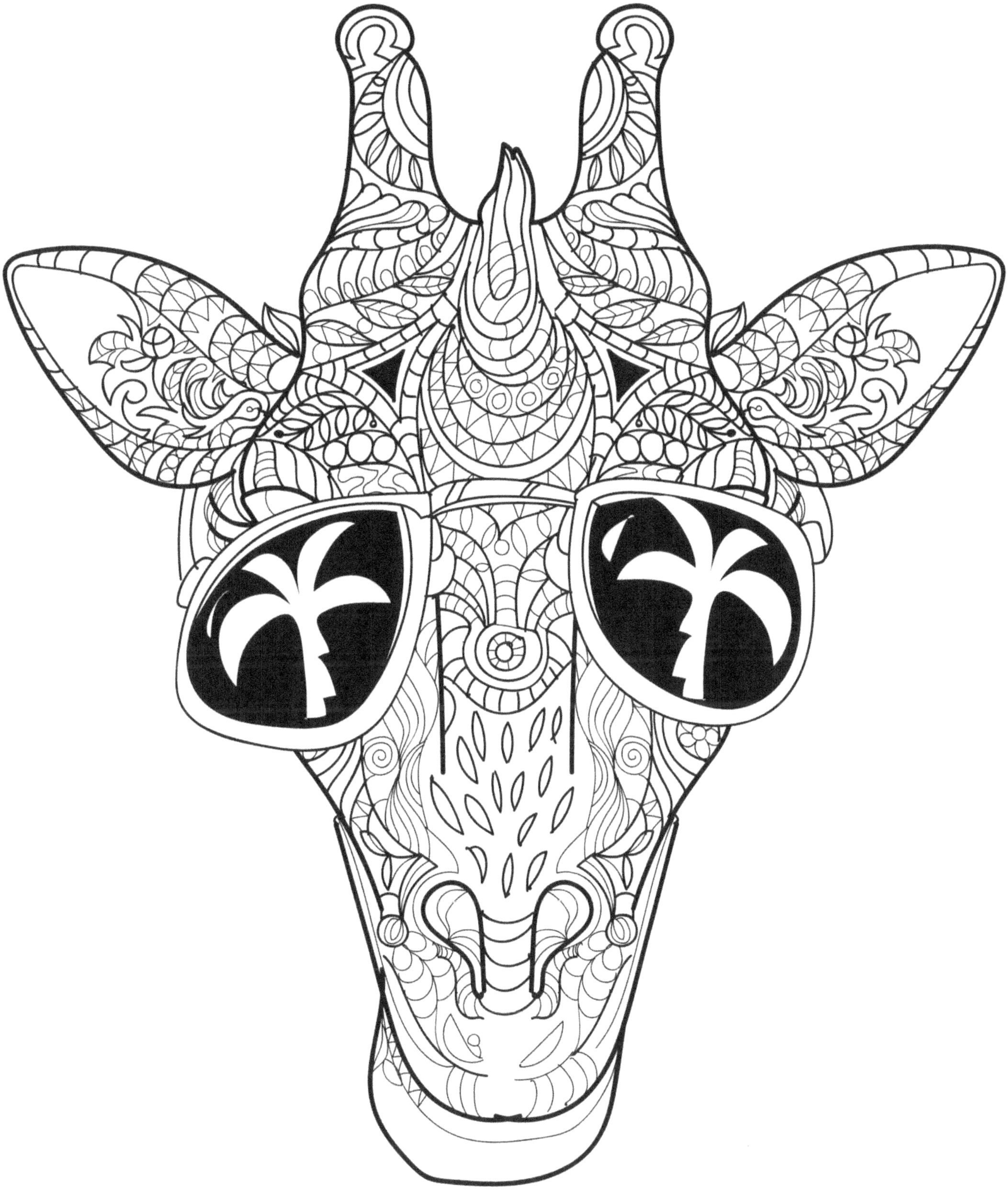

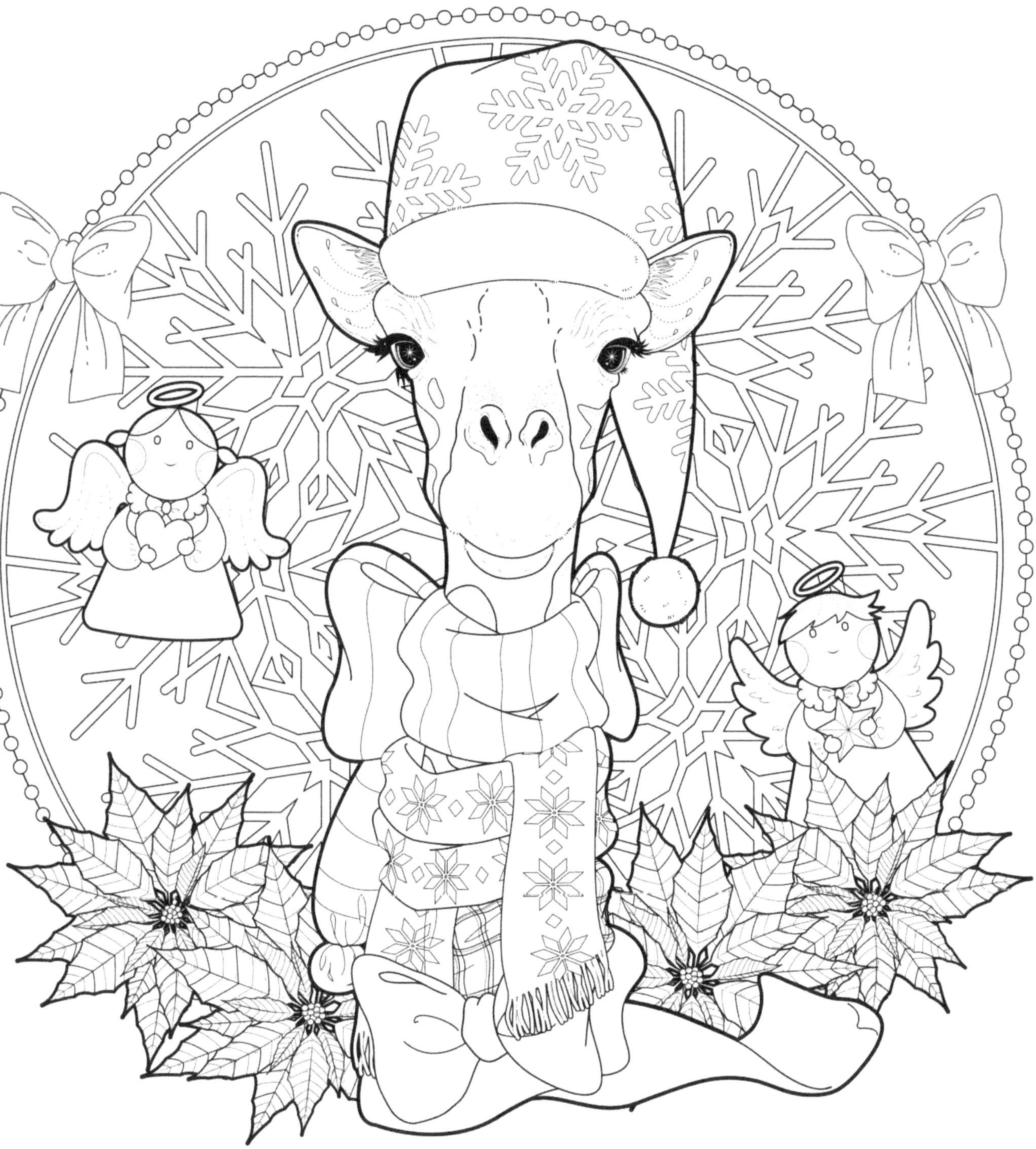

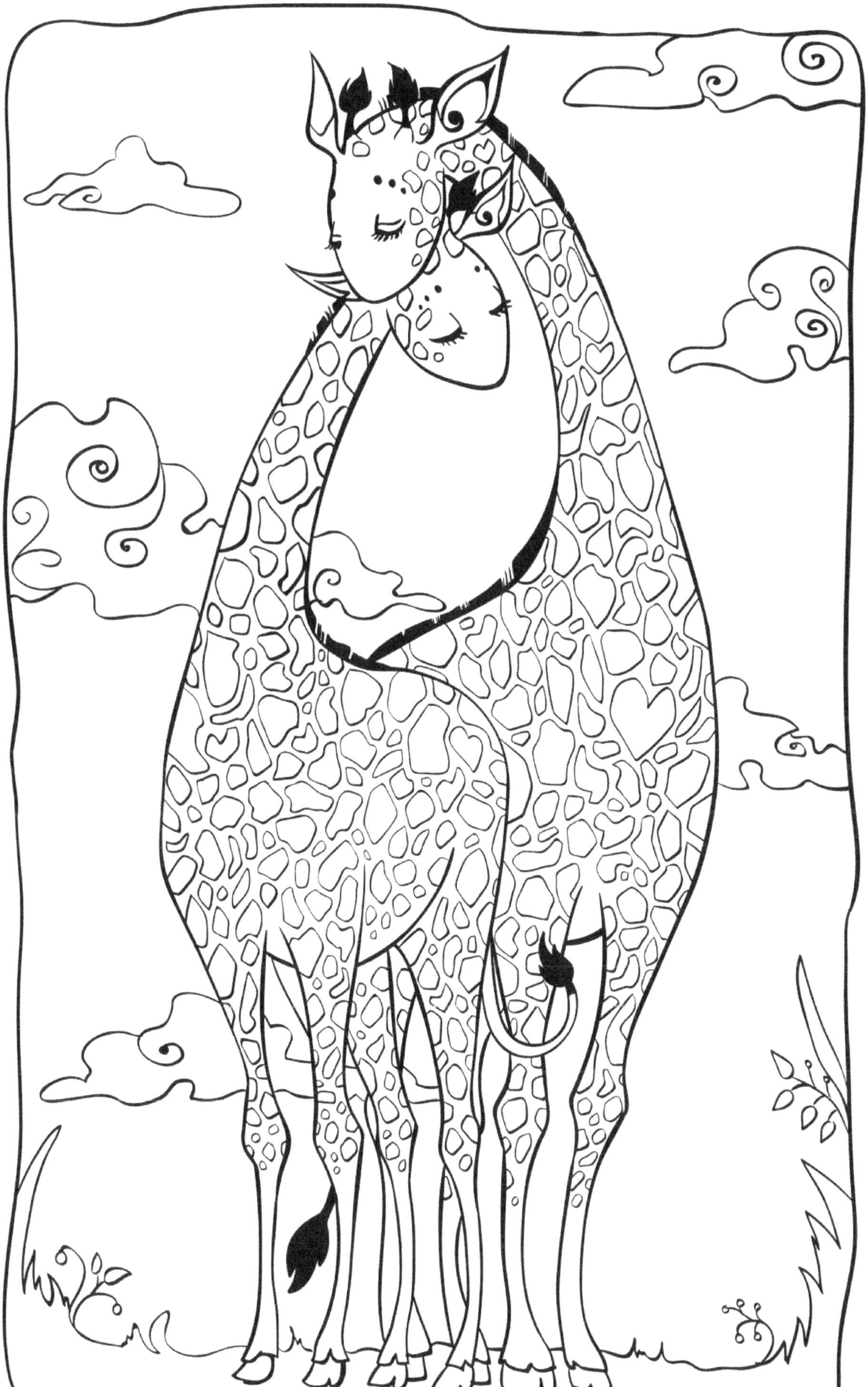

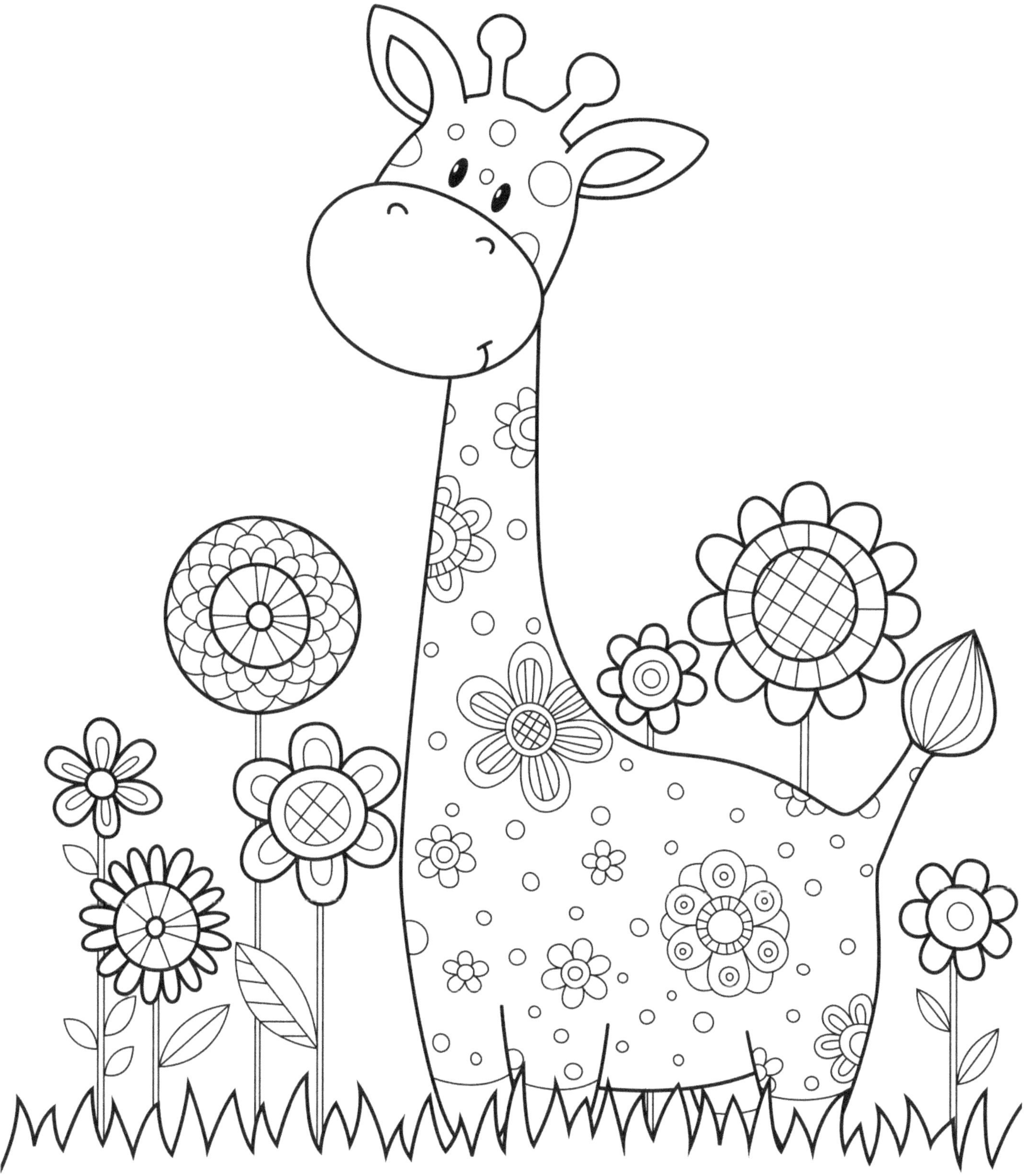

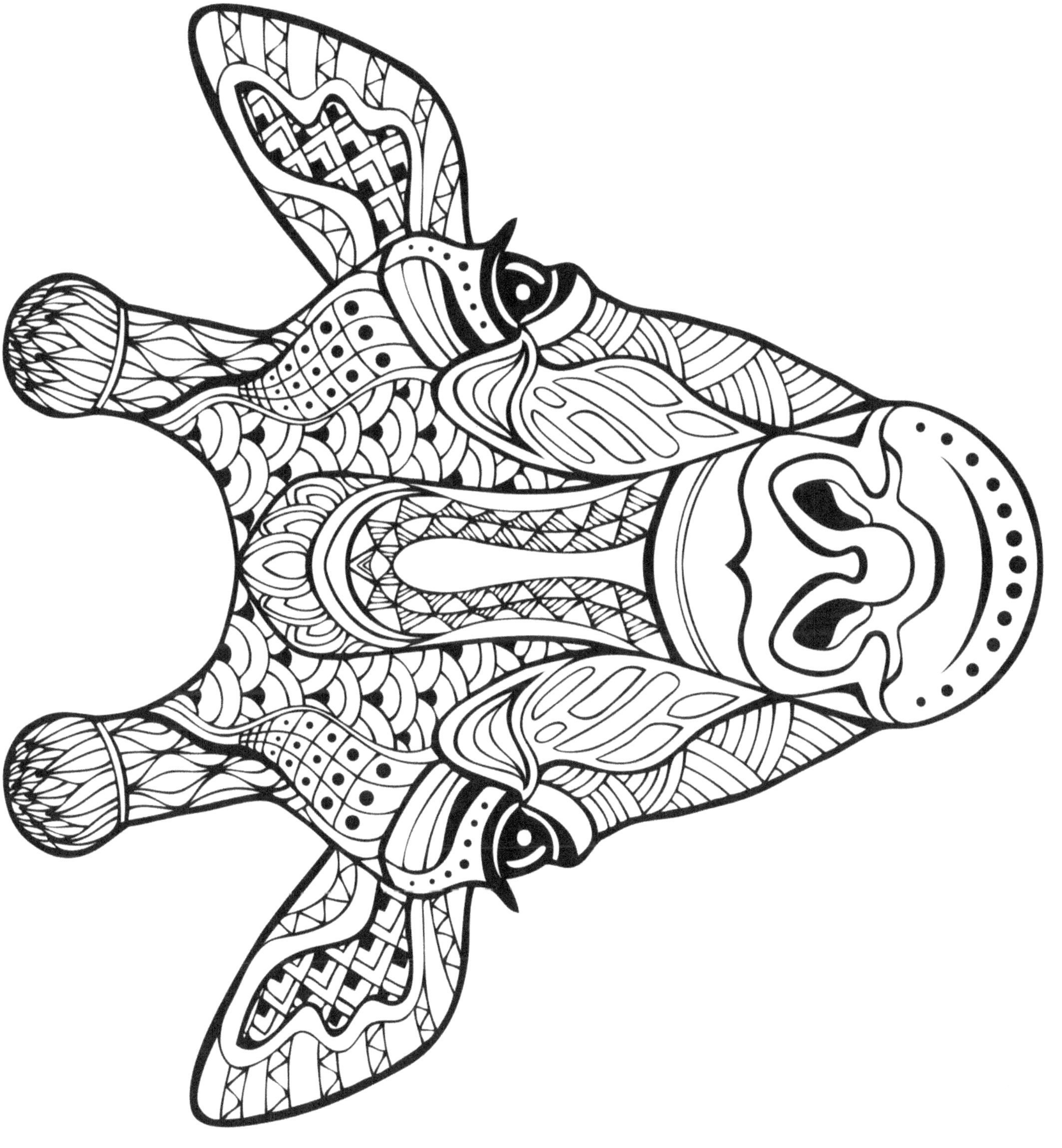

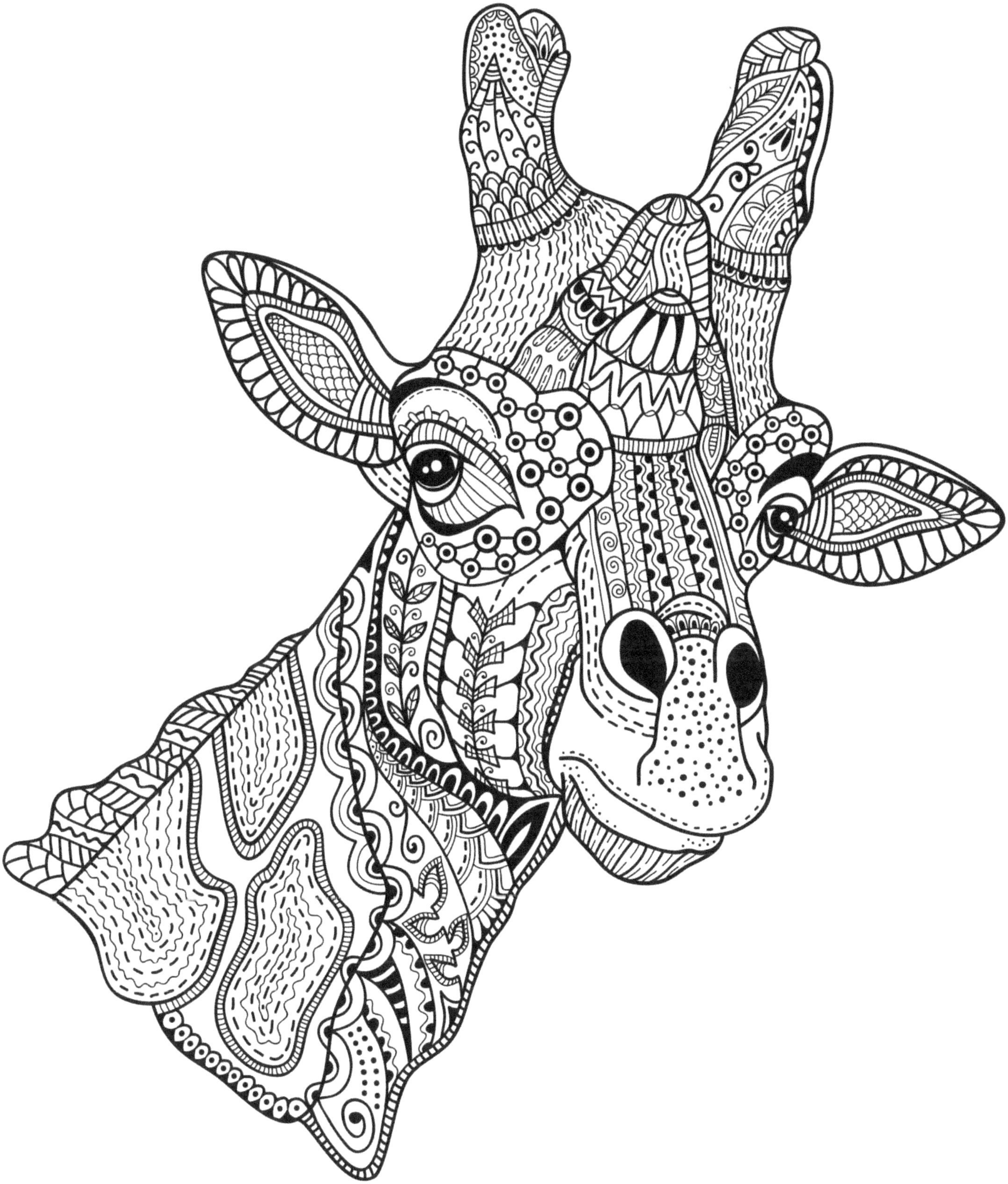

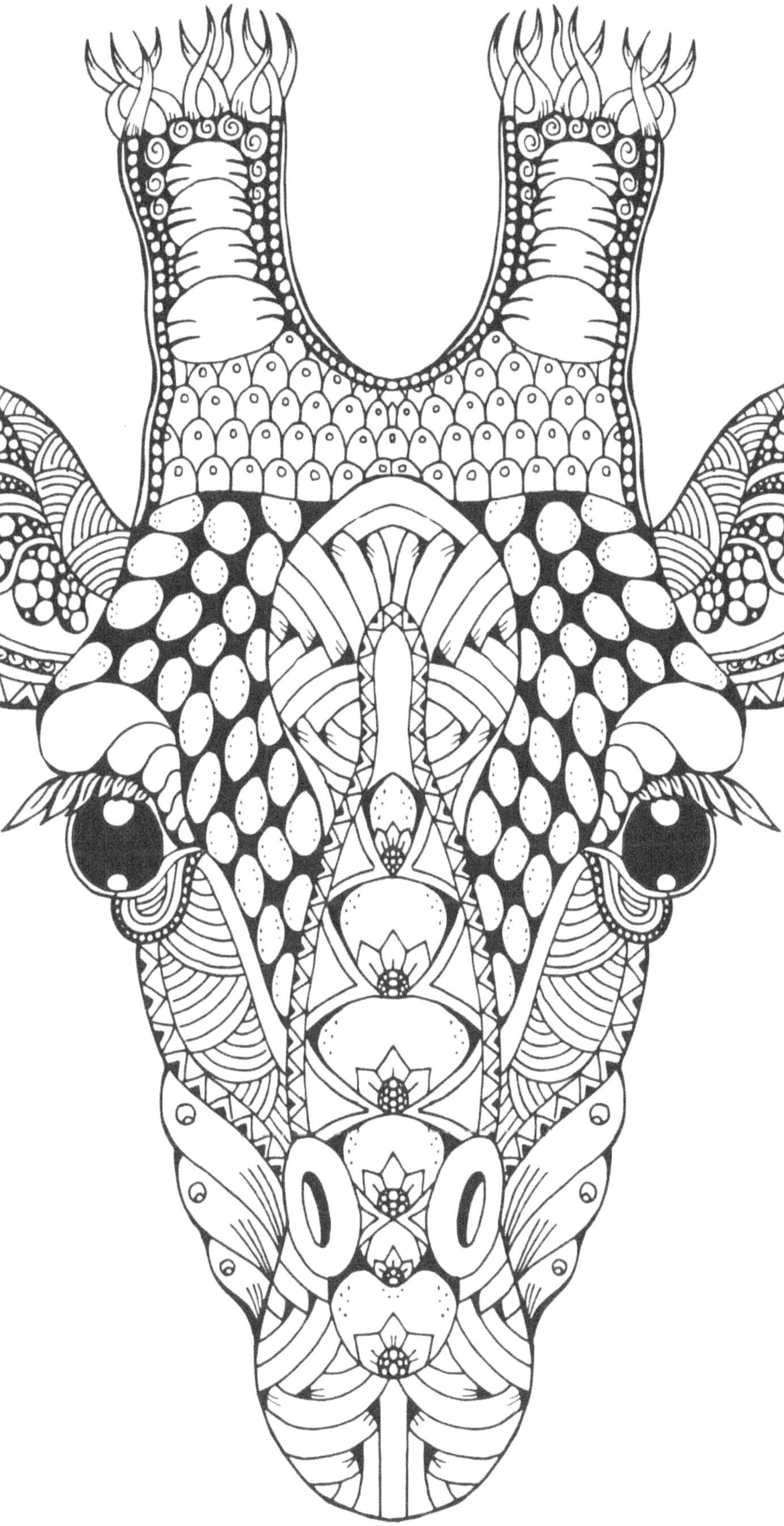

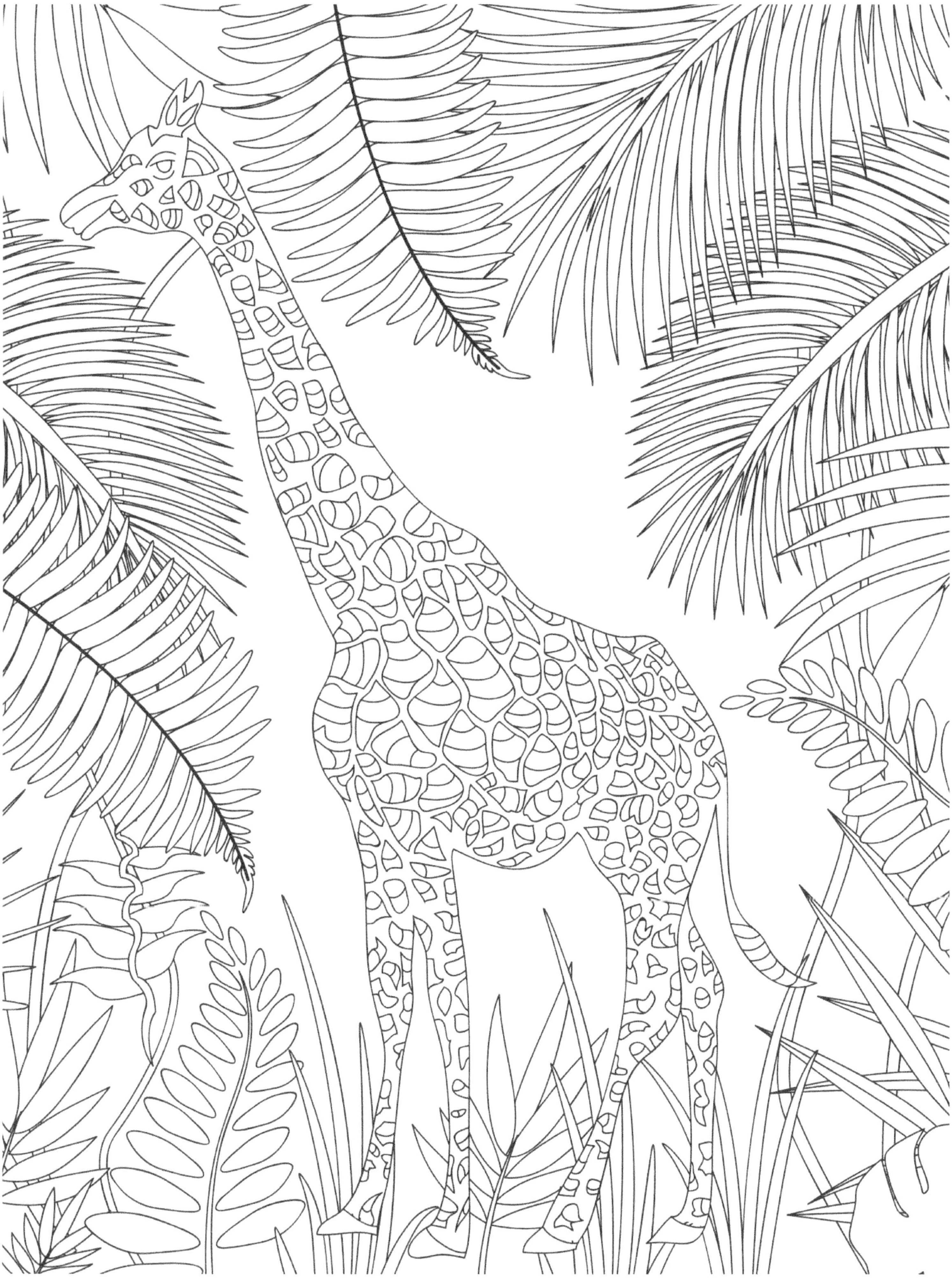

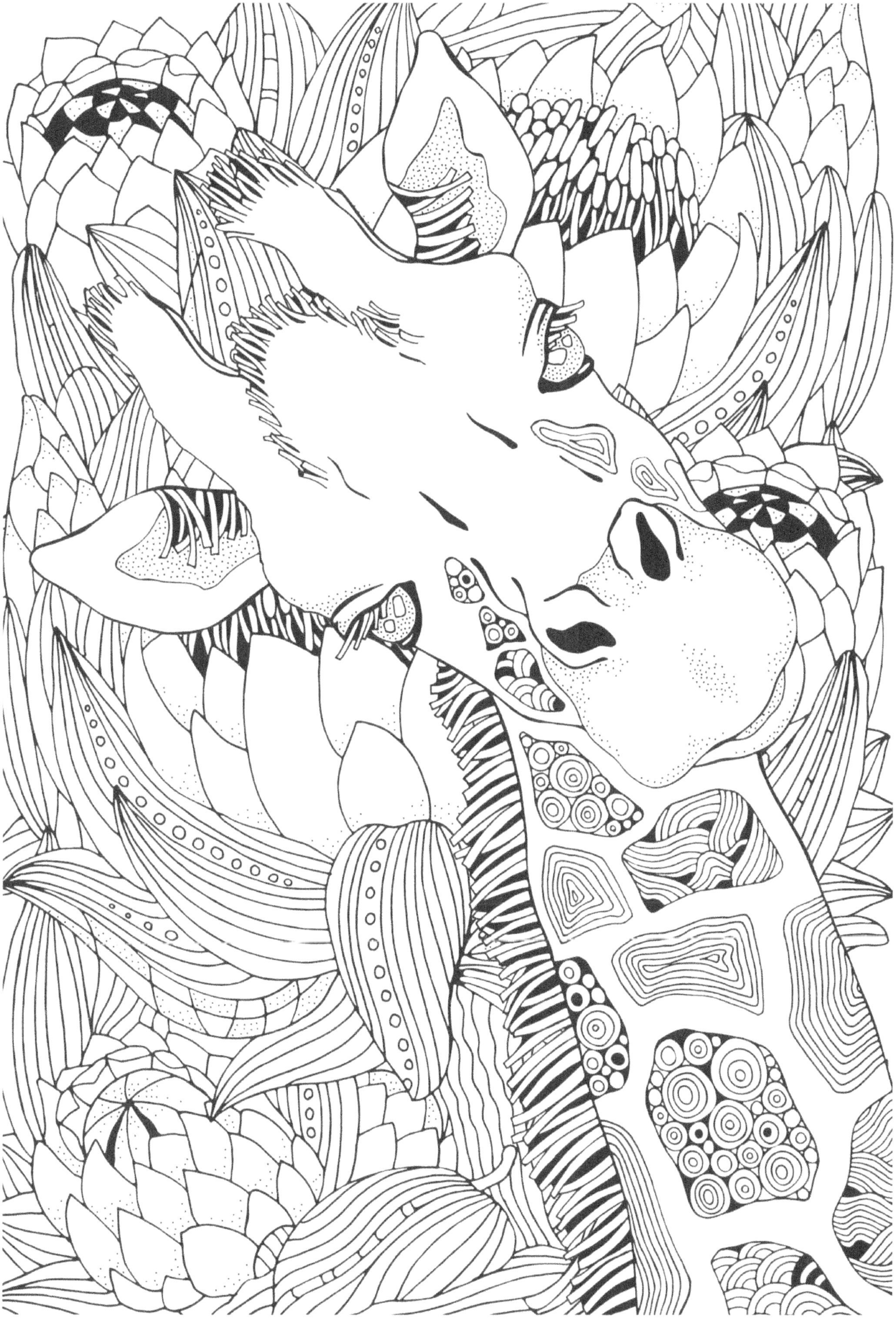

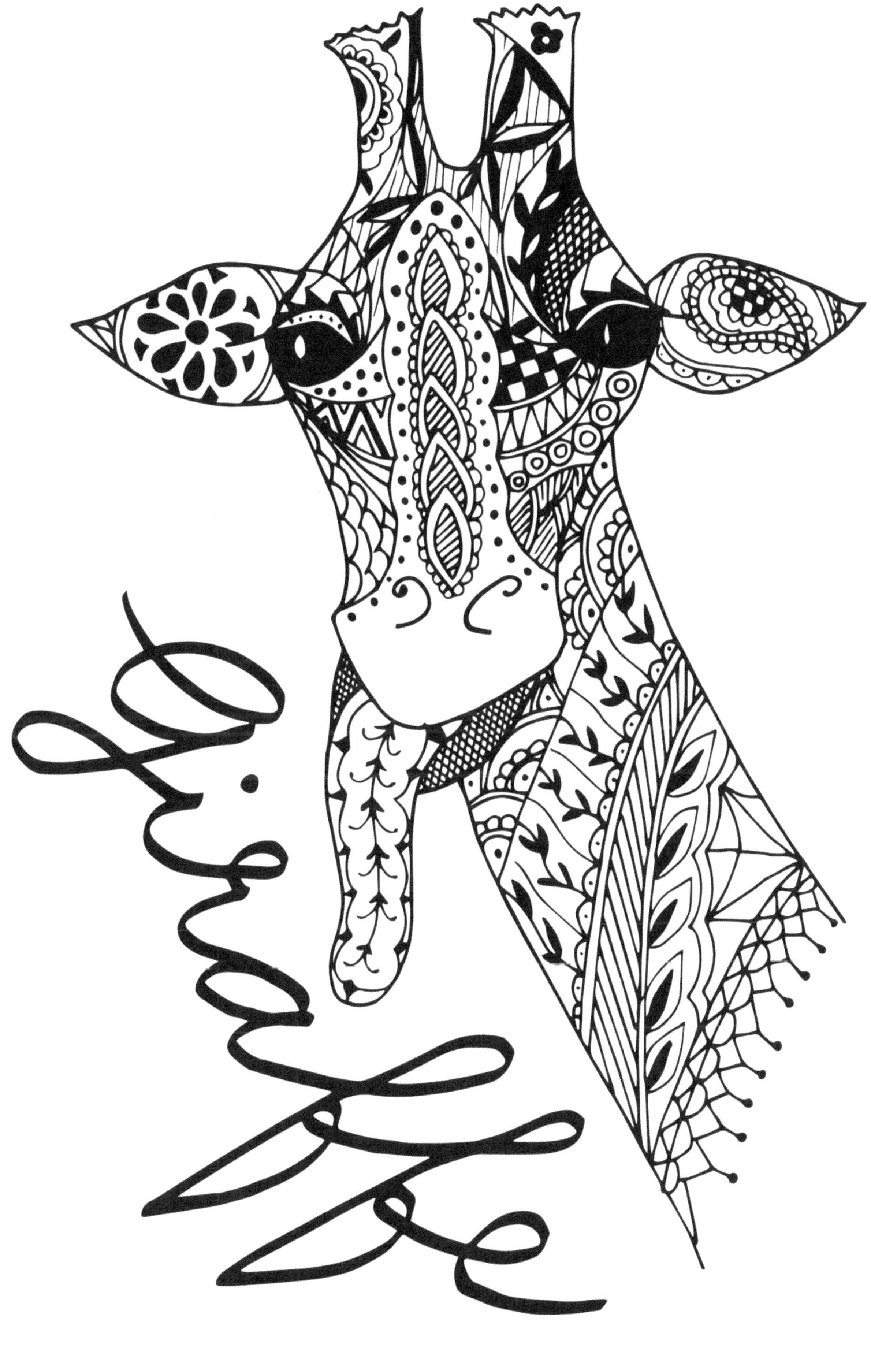
Giraffe

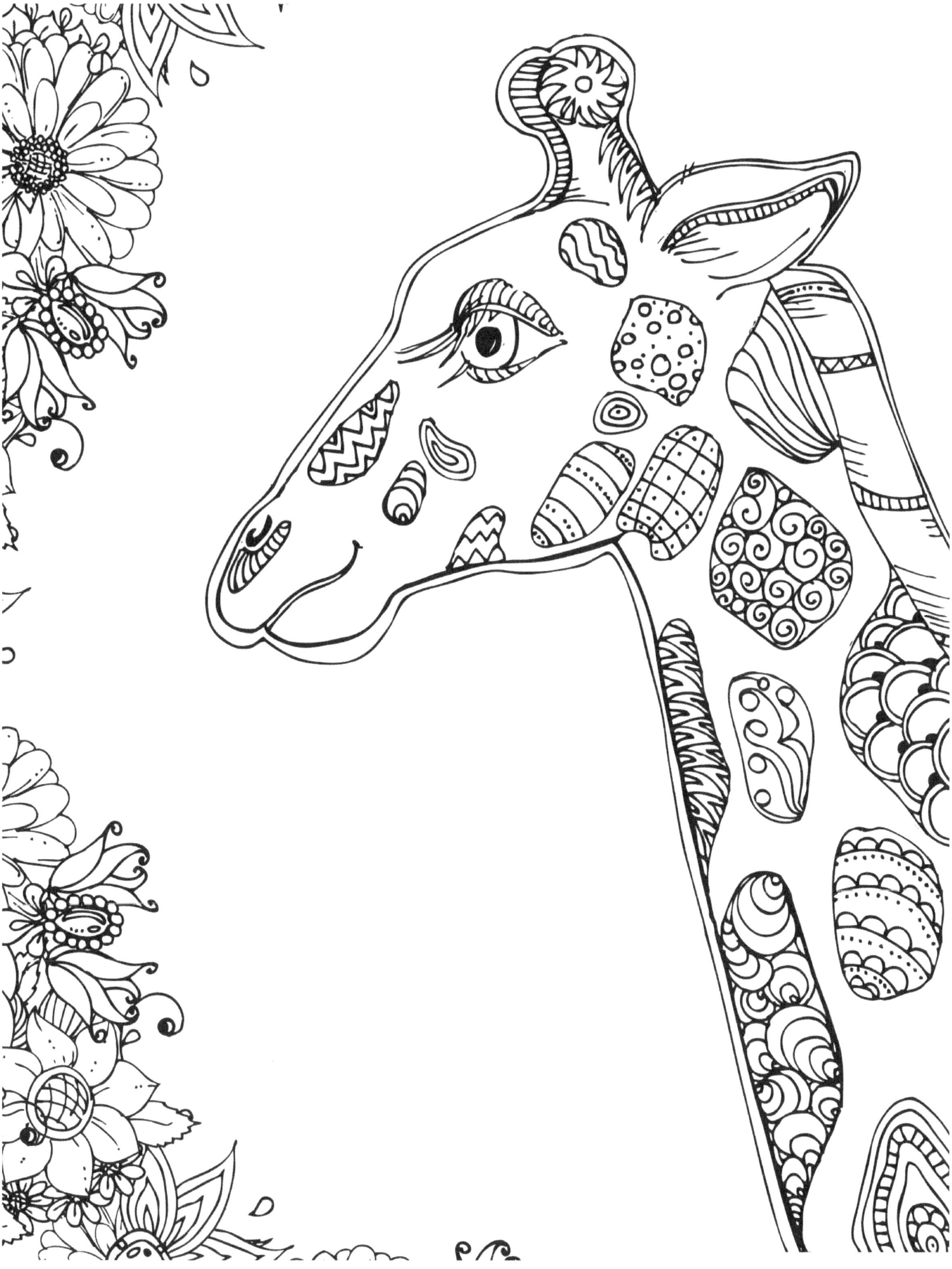

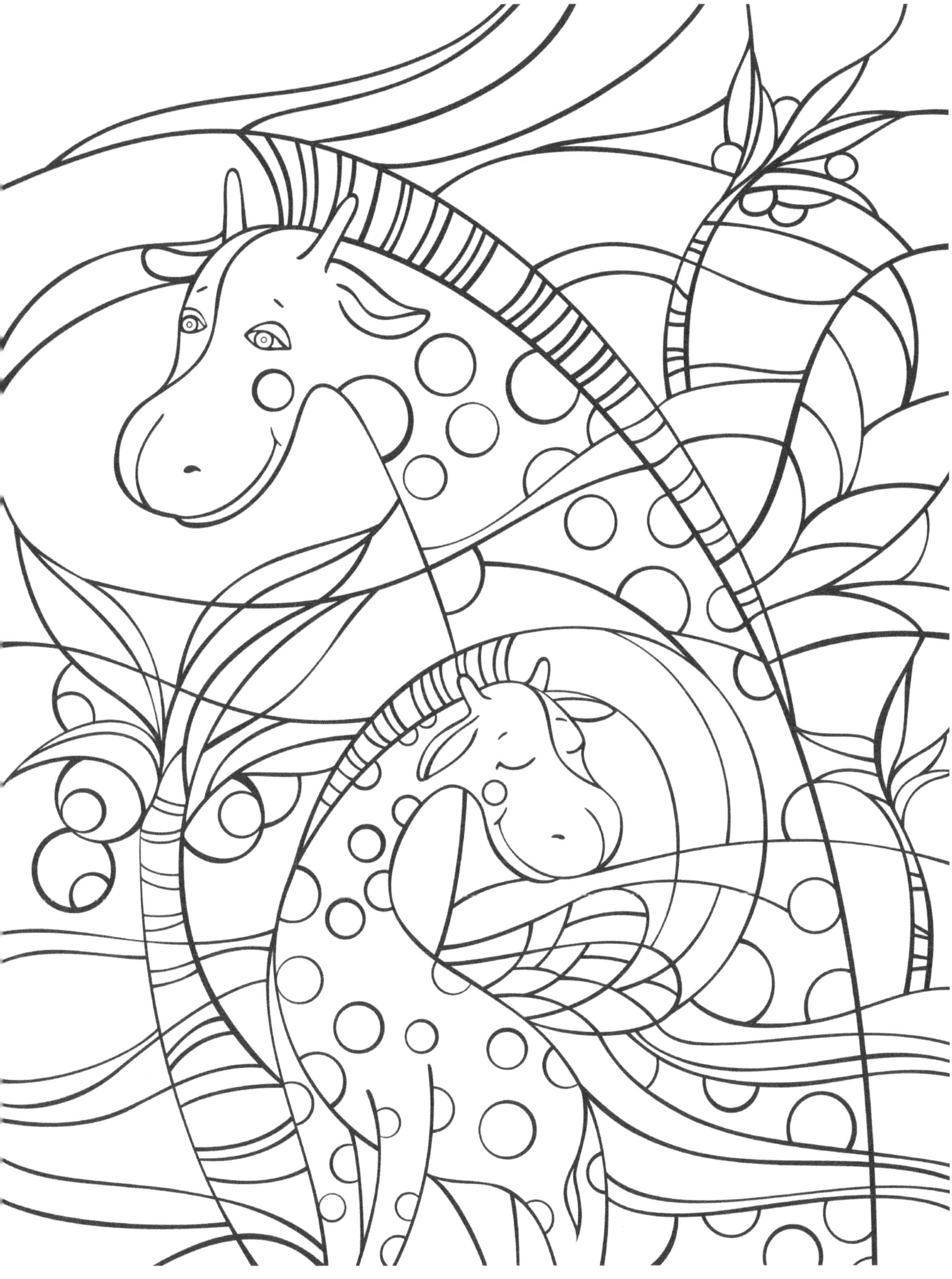

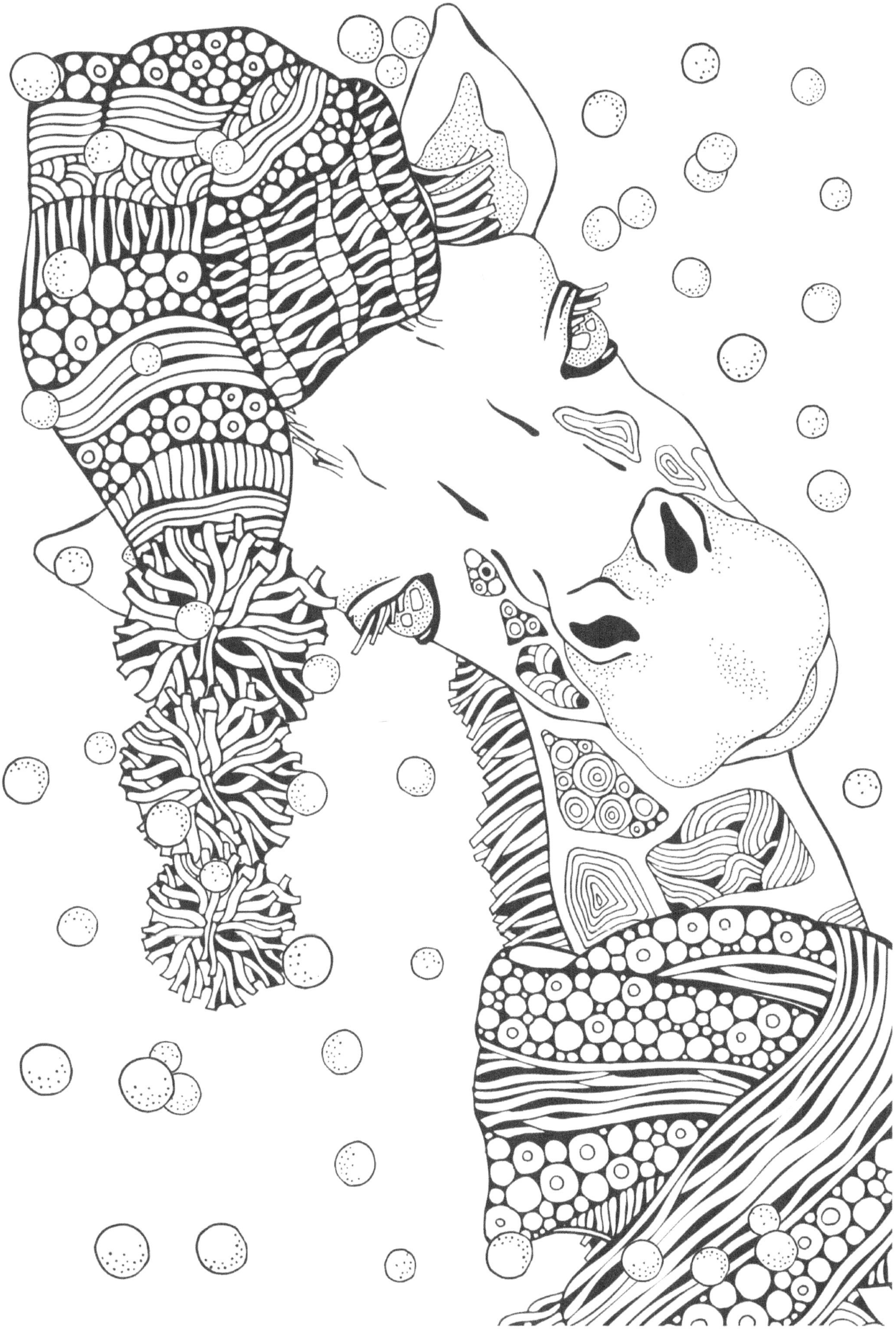

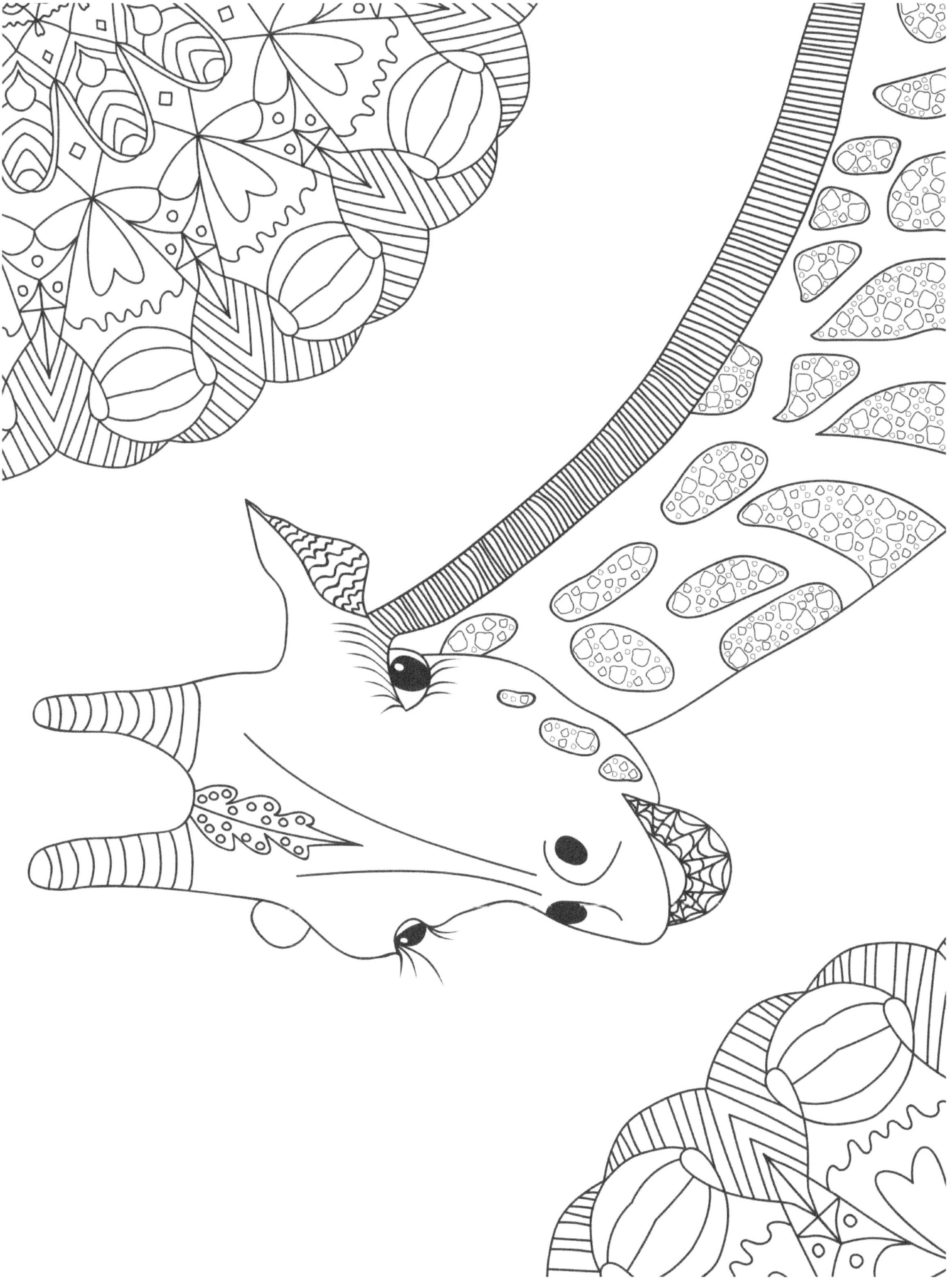

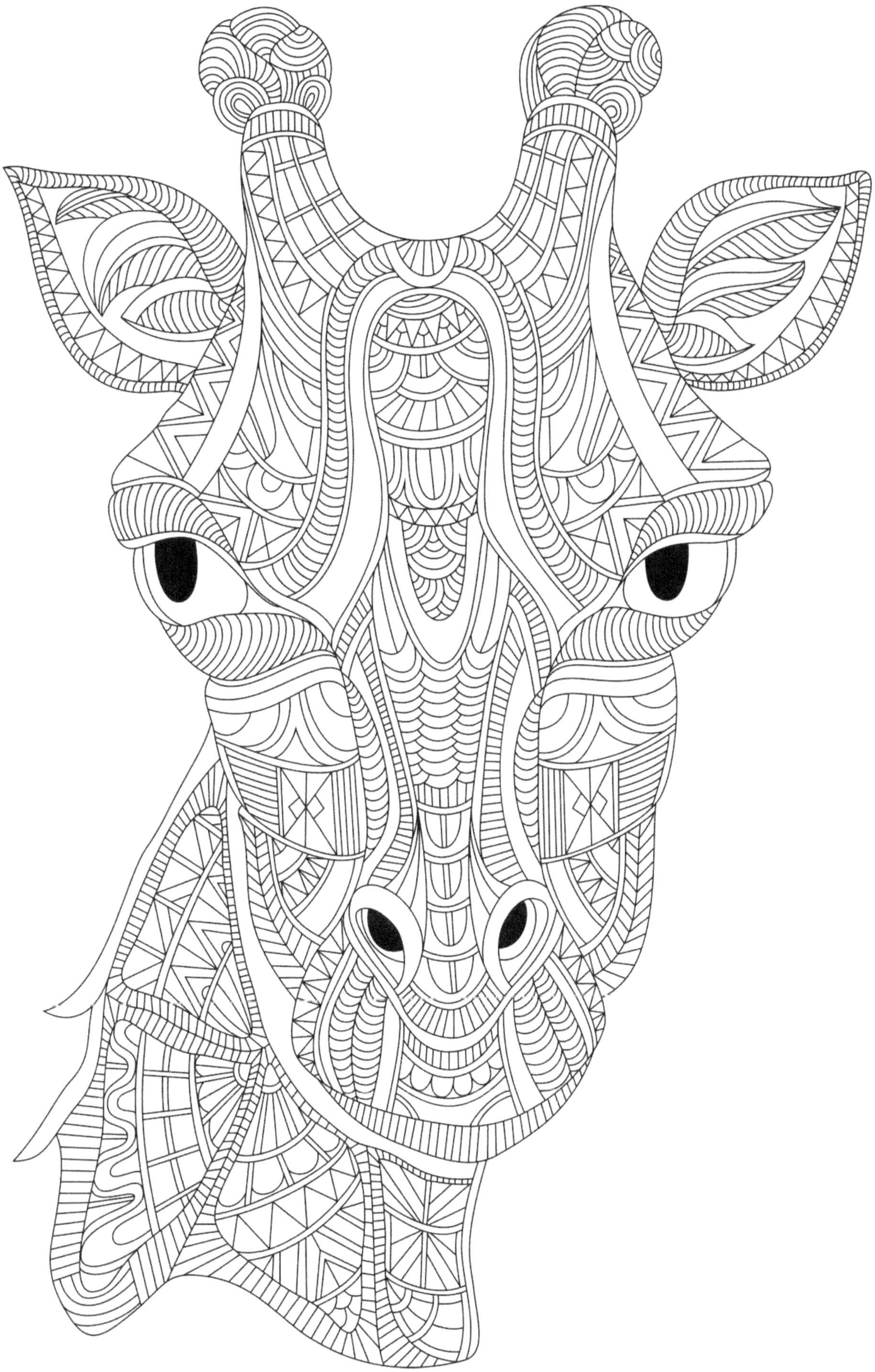

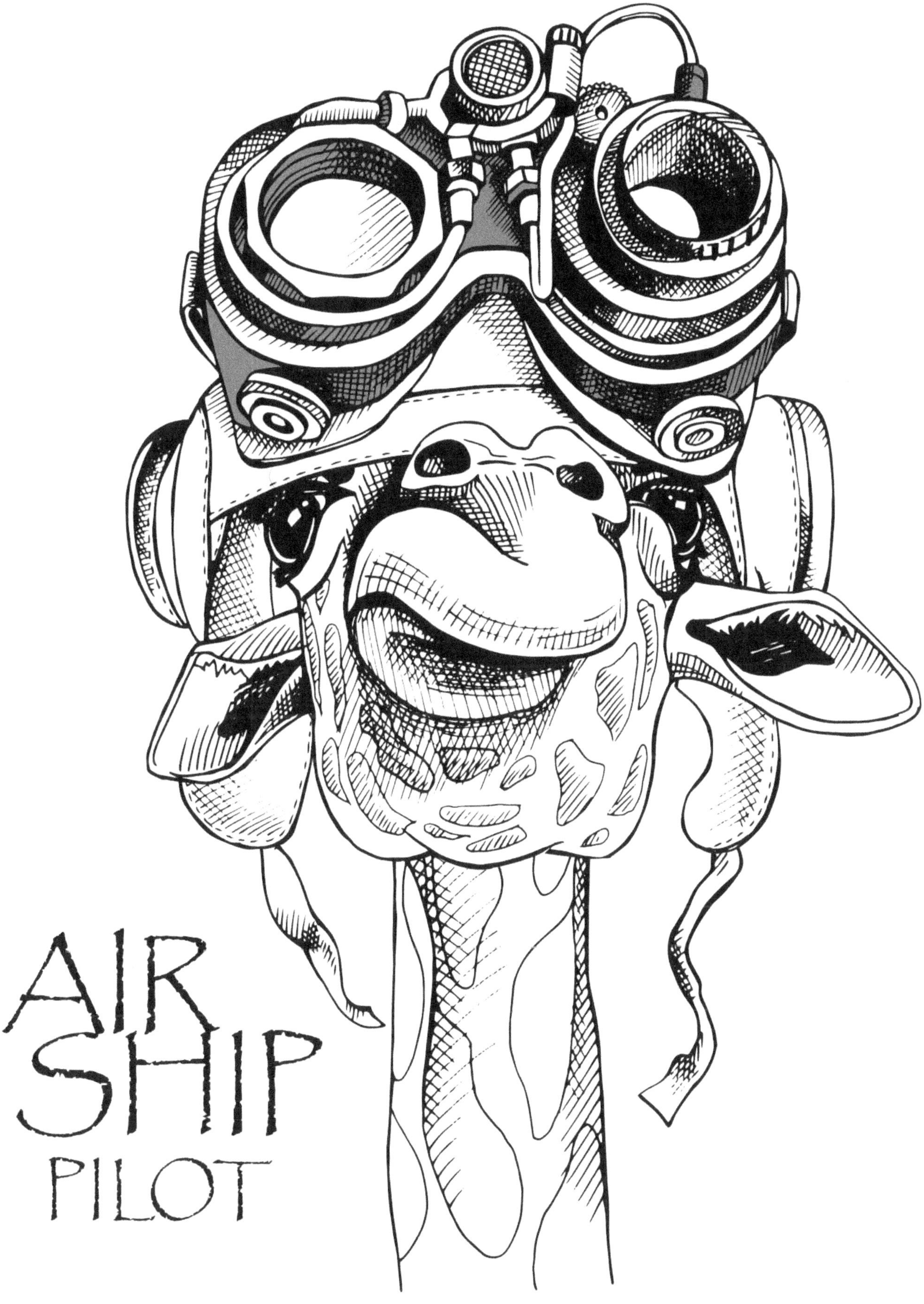
AIR
SHIP
PILOT

www.ingramcontent.com/pod-product-compliance
Lightning Source LLC
Chambersburg PA
CBHW081018240526
45471CB00017B/3412
9781986139007